W9-CHL-208

S 14208                    320.3
                           RAY

Raymond Thomas

DISCARD

Politics, power, and people

*Politics, Power, and People*

# POLITICS, POWER, AND PEOPLE

*Four Governments in Action*

*by Thomas Raynor*

*Franklin Watts*
*New York/London/Toronto*
*Sydney/1983*

36660000004456

*Library of Congress Cataloging in Publication Data*

*Raynor, Thomas P.*
*Politics, power, and people.*

*Bibliography: p.*
*Includes index.*
*Summary: Discusses the various ways of organizing*
*power in society, explores the philosophical foundations*
*of democracy, oligarchy, and other forms of government,*
*and compares the governments of the United Kingdom, the*
*United States, the Soviet Union, and Argentina.*
*1. Comparative government—Juvenile literature.*
*[1. Comparative government. 2. Political science.*
*3. Power (Social sciences)] I. Title.*
*JF127.R39    1983            320.3            83-10614*
*ISBN 0-531-04662-1*

*Copyright © 1983 by Thomas Raynor*
*All rights reserved*
*Printed in the United States of America*
*5   4   3   2   1*

320.3
RAY

# Contents

S14208

**PART III
PEOPLE AND POLITICS:
FOUR GOVERNMENTS
IN ACTION**

**PART IV
CONCLUSION**

*Politics, Power, and People*

**1**

The
Problem
of
Power

# 1

## Introduction: A Debate Among Conspirators

*I will make you shorter by the head.*

*Elizabeth I,*
*Queen of England, 1558–1603*

*The Queen turned crimson with fury,*
*and after glaring at her for a moment*
*like a wild beast, began screaming,*
*"Off with her head! Off with . . ."*

*Lewis Carroll,*
*Alice's Adventures in*
*Wonderland, 1865*

*If you do not obtain confessions,*
*we will shorten you by a head.*

*Joseph Stalin,*
*General Secretary of the*
*Communist Party of the*
*Soviet Union, 1927–1953*

One of society's nightmares, in both fact and fantasy, has been the fear of absolute power. Absolute power is the power of life and death over others. Where rulers exercise absolute power, subjects live in fear and dread.

Power is strength. Power is the ability to influence the behavior of others, getting them to do what they might not otherwise do. Those who have power can decide how the resources of society—goods, services, privileges—will be divided. They can decide who gets what, and when. Very early in its history, every society must decide who should have power over whom, and how those who have power can be prevented from gaining absolute power.

Government is a way of organizing power in society. It is a way of distributing power among individuals, and holding those individuals responsible for the way they use their power. In forming governments, societies decide who should rule, how much power rulers should have, what the rights of individuals should be, and what the goals of power should be.

Since the time of ancient Greece, people have debated the merits of various kinds of government, asking which form of government is most effective and least abusive; asking who is best fit to rule society—a king, a group, or the people.

## THE DEBATE BEGINS

In ancient Persia, a group of noblemen assassinated their king. Through the brutal use of absolute power, the king had become a hated tyrant. Soon after the killing, three of the conspirators met to decide what form of government should replace the overthrown monarchy. Their debate was reconstructed by the Greek historian Herodotus and told in his *Histories*, which were published in the fifth century B.C.:

> The first speaker was Otanes, who argued for the formation of a democratic government—the rule of the people. Otanes was followed by Megabyzus, who rec-

ommended the principles of oligarchy, the rule of a few. Darius was the third to speak, and he favored restoring the monarchy.

*Otanes:*
I think the time has passed for any one man to have absolute power. Monarchy is neither pleasant nor good. How can monarchy be ethical when it allows a man to do whatever he likes without any responsibility or control?

Even the best of men raised to such a position would be bound to change for the worse; he could not possibly see things as he used to. The typical vices of a monarch are envy and pride: envy, because it is a natural human weakness, and pride, because excessive wealth and power lead to the delusion that he is something more than a man. These two vices are the root cause of all wickedness. Both lead to acts of savage and unnatural violence.

Contrast monarchy with democracy, the rule of the people. The people in power do none of the things that monarchs do. Under a government of the people, an official is selected by lot and held responsible for his conduct in office. All questions are put up for open debate. Finally, the rule of the people ensures equality before the law. For these reasons, I propose that we do away with monarchy and raise the people to power.

*Megabyzus:*
In so far as Otanes favors abolishing monarchy, I agree with him. But he is wrong in asking us to transfer power to the people. The masses are an irresponsible lot. Nowhere will you find more ignorance or violence. It would be an intolerable thing to escape the murderous caprice of a king, only to be caught by the equally wanton brutality of a mob. A king at least acts with deliberation, but the mob does not. Indeed how could it, when it has never been taught what is right and proper?

Let us choose a certain number of the best men in the country, and give *them* political power. It is only natural to suppose that the best men will produce the best decisions and policies.

*Darius:*
I support all that Megabyzus says about the masses, but I do not agree with what he said of oligarchy. In an oligarchy, the fact that a number of men are competing for distinction leads to violent personal feuds. Each of them wants to get to the top, and to see his own proposals adopted.

In a democracy, corrupt dealings in government services lead to close personal associations. Eventually these cliques gain control of the government. Finally somebody comes forward as the people's champion, breaking up the cliques which are out for their own interests. This wins him the admiration of the mob, and as a result, he soon finds himself entrusted with absolute power.

In a monarchy, there is one ruler. It is impossible to improve on that, provided that he is the best man for the job. His judgement will be in keeping with his character. His control of the people will be exercised with moderation. His measures against enemies and traitors will be kept secret more easily than under other forms of government. I maintain that monarchy is preferable to all other forms of government....

The outcome of the debate among the three conspirators was inconclusive. Otanes, Megabyzus, and Darius found it no easier to agree on the ideal form of government than people do today. The problem of power has never been resolved once and for all.

## THE GREEKS JOIN THE DEBATE

The ancient Greeks were the first to denounce tyranny as a form of government, emphasizing instead the participation of the people in government. The Greeks were the first to develop the idea of constitutionalism, or rule by law. They were also the first to study government systematically.

Plato and Aristotle developed a sixfold classification of governments that is still useful today. The classification includes three "true," or constitutional, states, in which rulers rule for the good of all; and three "perverted," or despotic, states, in which rulers govern in the interest of the ruling class.

|  | Constitutional form of government | Despotic form of government |
| --- | --- | --- |
| Rule by one individual | Monarchy | Tyranny |
| Rule by a small group | Aristocracy | Oligarchy |
| Rule by the people | Democracy | Mob rule |

## THE DEBATE CONTINUES

This book is a continuation of the debate on government that began more than two thousand years ago. It describes and compares four governments—those of the United Kingdom, the United States, the Soviet Union, and Argentina. Of these four governments, two are democracies and two are oligarchies. One of the two democracies, the United Kingdom, has a parliamentary system of government. The other, the United States, has a presidential system. Of the two oligarchies, one—the Soviet Union—has a communist government ruled by a single party. The other, Argentina, has a military government ruled by a junta—a group of officers representing the armed forces.

Chapter Two explores the philosophical foundations of democracy, oligarchy, and other forms of government. It identifies the questions about power that all societies must answer—who should rule, what the limits of power should be, what the rights of individuals should be, and what the goals of power should be.

Chapter Three explains why it is that each society answers these questions about power differently, and why a society chooses one form of government rather than another. Chapters Four through

Seven trace the historical development of the governments of the United Kingdom, the United States, the Soviet Union, and Argentina, explaining why each of these countries chose the form of government they chose.

Chapters Eight through Eleven describe and compare the four governments in action, as they deal with the questions about power on a day-by-day basis. Chapter Twelve offers final conclusions.

Why study and compare governments? Because learning more about other governments gives us a better understanding not only of other societies, but about our own society and government, with all their strengths and weaknesses. Through such comparisons we come closer to realizing what the Greeks considered the goal of all learning—self-knowledge.

# 2

## Power: Five Questions, Two Traditions

*Still one more thing, fellow citizens
—a wise and frugal government,
which shall restrain men from injuring
one another, which shall leave them
otherwise free to regulate their own
pursuits of industry and improvement,
and shall not take from the mouth
of labor the bread it has earned.
This is the sum of good government.*

*Thomas Jefferson,
first inaugural address, 1801*

*The principle that society exists
solely for the well-being and the
personal liberty of all the individuals
of which it is composed is not
consistent with the plans of nature . . .
Fascism denies the absurd untruth
of political equality dressed up in the
garb of collective irresponsibility.*

*Benito Mussolini, 1925*

**G**overnment is the organization and distribution of power among rulers and institutions. It is a system for making laws and decisions that affect everyone in society. There are basically two traditions of government—democracy, which is government by many or all of the people; and authoritarianism, which is government by a single person or a few. These two conflicting traditions rest on conflicting views of human nature that were first put forth by two English philosophers of the seventeenth century and a French philosopher of the eighteenth.

According to one of the English philosophers, Thomas Hobbes (1588–1679), life without government means "no arts, no letters, no society; and worst of all, continual fear and danger of violent death." Being "nasty and brutish" by nature, said Hobbes, people behave foolishly, selfishly, and aggressively. Without a powerful ruler, they would destroy themselves. Recognizing their common danger, they agree to delegate unlimited power to a ruler who will keep peace and order.

The other Englishman, John Locke (1632–1704), saw things differently. Because freedom, equality, and independence are "natural," or God-given, rights, said Locke, "no one can be subjected to the political power of another without his own consent." Locke believed that people are generally good, intelligent, and reasonable. But conflicts arise among them, and some individuals threaten the rights of others. To satisfy the need for a "common judge," people form states, which are political communities, and governments. They make an agreement, or "social contract," with their rulers, stating that "the great and chief end" of government is to preserve the lives, liberties, and property of its citizens. If a government destroys people's rights, said Locke, the social contract is broken and the people have a right to change their government.

The French philosopher Jean-Jacques Rousseau (1712–1778) gave Locke's theory of the social contract a twist. Rousseau said that sovereignty, or supreme power, belongs to the people. Departing from Locke's idea of the social contract, Rousseau argued that individuals must obey the state because the state embodies "the general will of the people." In other words, once the state is formed, according to Rousseau, it sometimes knows better than the people themselves where their interests lie. In obeying the state, said Rousseau, we are obeying ourselves. Because he exalts the state over the people, Rousseau is sometimes seen as the forerunner of modern proponents of authoritarian governments.

The theories and arguments of Hobbes, Locke, and Rousseau are the foundations of modern democracy and authoritarianism. Like Hobbes, authoritarians today argue that people are not fit to govern themselves. With Rousseau, they claim that "the party" or the army represents "the general will of the people." Like Locke, democrats assert that rulers derive their limited powers from the sovereignty, or supreme power, of consenting citizens.

From these conflicting premises, democrats and authoritarians have developed two distinct responses to the questions about power and government that confront every society.

## WHO SHOULD RULE?

Authoritarians favor the concentration of power in a single ruler or select group, called an elite. Hobbes, who lived during the reign of Elizabeth I of England, supported the monarchy, which claimed absolute power as a right granted by God—a "divine right." According to this view of government, the king possesses supreme power and is often described as "the sovereign." Louis XIV of France was asserting the theory of divine right when he said to his parliament, "I am the state."

Modern authoritarians have more or less rejected the claim of divine right, as well as monarchy. Instead, they argue that one group deserves power—the Fascist Party or the Communist Party or the army, for example—because it knows the interests of the people better than they themselves do. Authoritarians believe the people are not yet able to govern themselves, and may never be. According to the German fascist Adolf Hitler, "A majority can never replace one man. Just as a hundred fools do not make one wise man, a heroic decision is not likely to come from a hundred cowards."

Democrats strongly disagree. "No man is good enough to govern any other man without that other's consent," said Abraham Lincoln. Democrats insist that the people are sovereign and ought to govern themselves. "Sometimes it is said that man cannot be trusted with the government of himself," Thomas Jefferson wrote. "Can he then be trusted with the government of others?" In a true democracy, the people exercise their sovereignty directly, participating in all decisions. In a representative democracy, or republic, the people delegate authority to representatives who are held accountable by law and through elections.

## WHAT ARE THE LIMITS OF POWER?

Some authoritarians recognize limits on their power; others do not. The great monarchs of Europe were absolutists who claimed the power of life and death over their subjects. They argued that if God himself had given them their power, then humans could not limit that power. But most of Europe's absolute monarchs came to regard certain social activities—religion and business, for example—as purely private matters. It was a minister of Louis XIV who developed the theory of *laissez-faire*, or "hands off" the economy.

Today there are authoritarian governments such as military dictatorships that seldom interfere in religion, the economy, or the affairs of other powerful groups in society. These governments are sometimes described as "conservative" because they aim only to prevent society from changing. They want to preserve the existing balance among social groups. But like all authoritarians, their rulers do not recognize limits imposed by law or the people. Whatever limits they observe are largely self-defined.

Hitler's Nazi government and the communist governments of the Soviet Union and its satellites have been described as "radical" because they seek to remake society, changing the existing balance of social forces. Often these governments recognize no limits at all, assuming control over education, religion, the economy, and even the arts and entertainment. Because they seek total control over society, these governments are also described as "totalitarian."

Democrats agree with John Locke that "wherever law ends, tyranny begins." They believe that the power of rulers is limited by law—ideally, by a constitution that defines the power of rulers and the rights of individuals. As Jefferson saw it, the rightful powers of government are limited indeed. And there is a simple test of their legality:

*—12*

The legitimate powers of government extend to such acts only as are injurious to others. But it does me no injury for my neighbor to say there are twenty gods, or no god. It neither picks my pocket nor breaks my leg.

In practice, Jefferson's test is difficult to apply. Democrats have always disagreed among themselves in defining the boundaries of governmental power. But they do agree that government derives its powers from the people; and that the people may limit those powers as they see fit.

## WHAT ARE THE RIGHTS OF INDIVIDUALS?

The rights of individuals are, at the same time, limits on the power of rulers. Democrats believe that individual rights are "natural," or God-given: "The God who gave us life," wrote Jefferson, "gave us liberty at the same time." Individual rights are therefore "unalienable," said Jefferson—no government can rightfully deny them.

Those who framed the U.S. Constitution spelled out the powers of the president, the Congress, and the courts, but not all of the individual rights that the new government would be required to respect. When Jefferson received a draft of the Constitution in Paris, where he was serving as the American ambassador, he objected most strongly to this omission. His objection was widely shared, and a major argument against the Constitution was the absence of a "bill of rights." Only after it was agreed that the new government's first order of business would be to adopt a Bill of Rights was the Constitution assured of ratification.

The Bill of Rights lists the inalienable rights of Americans, among them free speech, freedom of religious belief, and the right to a free press. In addition, it expresses the basic democratic belief that even those who are suspected of terrible crimes possess rights that no government can deny—the right to a trial, for example.

Authoritarians reject the claim that individuals possess natural or inalienable rights. With Hobbes, they argue that individuals derive whatever rights they possess from the government. Benito Mussolini, the founder of Italian Fascism, expressed the authoritarian view in these words:

—13

The foundation of Fascism is the conception of the state, its character, its duty, and its aim. Fascism conceives of the state as an absolute, in comparison with which all individuals or groups are relative, only to be conceived of in their relation to the state.

## WHAT SHOULD BE
## THE GOALS OF POWER?

The ideas of Hobbes, Locke, and Rousseau shaped the American and French revolutions. With the old authoritarian governments overthrown, the French and the Americans faced the task of making democracy a reality. In the 1770s two young lawyers— one French, the other American—addressed the same basic question about power. What should it be used for? What should its purposes, or goals, be? The American, John Adams, wrote:

A constitution founded on these principles introduces knowledge among the people, and inspires them with a conscious dignity becoming free men; a general emulation takes place, which causes good humor, sociability and good manners to be general. That elevation of sentiment inspired by such a government makes the common people brave and enterprising. That ambition which is inspired by it makes them sober, industrious and frugal. You will find among them some elegance, perhaps, but more solidity; a little pleasure, but a great deal of business; some politeness, but more civility.

The Frenchman, Maximilien Robespierre, wrote:

In our country we desire morality instead of selfishness; honesty and not mere "honor"; principle and not mere custom; duty and not mere self-concern; the sway of reason rather than the tyranny of fashion; a scorn for vice and not contempt for the unfortunate... good men instead of good company, merit in place of intrigue, talent in place of mere cleverness, truth and not show, the charm of happiness and not the boredom of pleasure... in short, the virtues and miracles of a republic and not the vices and absurdities of a monarchy.

*—14*

Adams, like Locke before him, saw government as a kind of traffic cop, with just enough power to accompish its limited purpose. Robespierre, in the tradition of Rousseau, saw government as a social engineer, busily reforming human nature and human institutions.

But as Robespierre discovered during his brief rule of France's revolutionary government, ambitious goals require unlimited power. In his efforts to create "a moral republic," Robespierre became the first leader to use terrorism as an instrument of governing. Modern authoritarians, too, have discovered that unlimited goals require unlimited power. Russia's communists set out to create "a new communist man." Iran's Muslim fundamentalists want to harmonize society and government with their religious beliefs. In both cases, radical goals required absolute power. And absolute power destroyed whatever hopes and possibilities existed for democracy.

## TWO TRADITIONS

As the 1700s drew to a close, two traditions in government had been established—democracy and authoritarianism. The conflict between these two traditions would shape the history of the century to come. Thomas Jefferson foresaw this development and expressed it in the following words:

> Men by their constitution are naturally divided into two parties: (1) Those who fear and distrust the people, and wish to draw all powers from them into the hands of the higher classes. (2) Those who identify themselves with the people, have confidence in them, cherish and consider them as the most honest and safe . . . depository of the public interests.
>
> In every country these two parties exist; and in every one where they are free to think, speak, and write, they will declare themselves.

# *People and Power: How History Shaped Four Governments*

# 3
## Why No Two Governments Are Alike

*In the long run every government is the exact symbol of its people, with their wisdom and unwisdom.*

*Thomas Carlyle,*
*Scottish historian, 1795–1881*

*After all, anybody is as their land and air is. Anybody is as the sky is low or high, and the air heavy or clear, and anybody is as there is wind or no wind there. It is that which makes them and the arts they make, and the work they do, and the way they eat, and the way they drink, and the way they learn and everything.*

*Gertrude Stein,*
*American writer, 1874–1946*

**M**en and women do not rationally consider the arguments of Hobbes, Locke, and Rousseau and then decide to become democrats or authoritarians. Societies do not debate the merits of each argument and then adopt a democratic or authoritarian form of government. Instead each society's history shapes its beliefs about power and government and pushes it in a democratic or authoritarian direction. Because no two societies share the same history, no two societies share the same beliefs about power—about who should rule, and so on. And because no two societies' beliefs about power are quite the same, no two governments are alike.

The historical experience of the British and the Russians offers good examples of how history shapes beliefs about power and government. Britain has been secure from invasion since 1066. Security encouraged the growth and acceptance of limited government, for it is chiefly in times of emergency that governments claim absolute power. Security has also meant that Britain has seldom maintained a large standing army. Without an army, English kings lacked decisive force in dealing with their opponents. As a result, such groups as nobles and townspeople grew strong enough to challenge and balance the power of the king.

The Russians, by contrast, have rarely been secure. They have experienced countless invasions and occupations. Foreigners destroyed the earliest institutions of Russian democracy. These experiences reinforced the belief that survival requires a strong central government with absolute power, as well as a powerful standing army and secret police. With forces such as these at their disposal, the Russian tsars were able to destroy challengers such as the powerful noble families. As a result, the Russian tsar became an absolute ruler.

Because their histories were so different, the Russians and the British developed very different beliefs about government. So it is with every society. A unique history shapes a unique set of beliefs about power and government that most members of society come to share. These shared beliefs about power and government are called "political culture."

Political culture represents a consensus of beliefs, including beliefs about who should rule; what limits should be placed on the power of leaders, if any; what individual rights and freedoms are inalienable, if any; and what the goals of power should be. In some societies the consensus is broad and deep. In others it is narrow and shallow. Whatever its characteristics, a unique political culture is the foundation on which every society builds a political system.

## POLITICAL SYSTEMS

A political system is an organized way of making decisions and resolving conflicts among the members of a society. Included in a modern political system are all of the following elements:

■  A government, which is the formal distribution of power among such institutions and leaders as congress, parliament, the president, and the courts. The government directs decision making in a society.

■  Political parties, which are a link between the government and the people. Parties present candidates for office. In a democracy, these candidates compete through elections for control of the government.

■  Interest groups, which represent the special goals of their members—businesspeople, workers, doctors, farmers, and others. Interest groups work to influence governments, parties, and voters.

■  The rules of politics, which is the competition for power. Rules may be written or unwritten; they may stem from law or tradition. They specify how individuals may become candidates for office, how candidates should compete, and how the choice among candidates is made. The rules also serve as norms that guide the behavior of elected and appointed officials.

■  The goals of the government, and its policies. Policies are action programs, or strategies, designed to achieve desired goals.

History shapes political culture, and political culture shapes each element of a political system—government, participants, rules, goals and policies. A society's political culture determines whether its political system will be democratic or authoritarian, whether it will be stable or unstable, whether or not the struggle for power can be kept within peaceful bounds, whether policies will favor the many or the few.

The chapters that follow in Part II trace the influence of history on the political cultures and political systems of the United Kingdom, the United States, the Soviet Union, and Argentina. In these societies, as in all other societies, historical events have played a greater role in shaping governments than the rational choices and preferences of the people.

# 4

# The United Kingdom: Commoners Against Kings

*It is atheism and blasphemy to dispute what God can do; so it is presumption and contempt to dispute what a king can do, or say that a king cannot do this or that.*

*James I, King of England, 1603–1625*

*The poorest man may in his cottage bid defiance to all the forces of the Crown. It may be frail, its roof may shake, the wind may blow through it, the storm may enter, the rain may enter —but the King of England cannot enter. All his force dares not cross the threshold of the ruined tenement.*

*William Pitt, British Prime Minister, 1757–1761*

**G**reat Britain is a geographical term describing the main island of the British Isles. Great Britain includes England, Scotland, and Wales, three countries that were unified by the kings of England between the thirteenth and eighteenth centuries.

In 1801, Great Britain and Ireland united to form the United Kingdom of Great Britain and Ireland. In 1921, when the Catholic counties of southern Ireland became independent as the Irish Free State, the union became known as the United Kindgom of Great Britain and Northern Ireland.

From prehistoric times until the Middle Ages, the British Isles were a destination and crossroads for countless tribes and traders of Europe. Great Britain was first settled by Celtic-speaking tribes from northern Europe in the sixth century B.C. In 57 B.C., Julius Caesar invaded the island, and Romans occupied it until 407 A.D., opening it to Roman trade and influence.

Among the greatest of Roman influences on English political culture was the Roman method of interpreting and applying laws. In Rome the chief judicial officer annually issued an edict indicating the rules he would apply in court. These rules soon became traditional, not only in Rome, but throughout the Roman Empire. As a result, law became independent of politics and the personal preferences of judges. The meaning of the law became predictable and consistent—the same for all. Historians believe that the development of a modern legal system rivals the political union of the Mediterranean world as the greatest achievement of the Roman Republic. Its influence on English political development was a decisive one.

## AFTER THE ROMANS

When the Romans withdrew from Great Britain, waves of Angles, Saxons, and Jutes moved in from Denmark and Germany, founding kingdoms which were overthrown by more Danish invaders in the eighth and ninth centuries. In 1016 a Dane, Canute, became king of a united Denmark and England.

The last successful invasion of Great Britain came fifty years later, from France. In 1066, Normans led by William the Conquerer subdued the English in the battle of Hastings, forever changing the course of British history and the shape of British society.

As king of England, William introduced Norman feudalism to this backward and fragmented society. He broke the power of the great lords, reducing them to vassals of the crown. In return for their pledge of loyalty and military service, the king promised his vassals justice and protection.

William laid the foundations for England's centralized monarchy. He created a Great Council consisting of nobles, land owners, and officials representing the king. Though it met infrequently and lacked decision-making powers, the Great Council was an early expression of the idea of representative government.

William's reign reinforced another important principle: the supremacy of the government over the church in affairs of state. William refused a loyalty oath to the pope and insisted on controlling the appointment of bishops and other church officials in England.

## THE MAGNA CARTA

Not since 1066 have the English experienced invasion and the disruption of society that invasions cause. Secure in their isolation, the English concentrated on developing sea power, which served for defense, as well as for the expansion of trade and empire. With no military tradition, English culture placed the highest value on civil and administrative skills. With no armies at their command, the English kings lacked the decisive force required to crush those who challenged their power.

One such challenge to royal power came in 1215. In that year, at Runnymede, noblemen forced King John to sign the Magna Carta, or great charter. In signing, John agreed that even the king must obey all the laws of the land.

The Magna Carta was the earliest modern expression of the idea of the rule of law, or constitutionalism. The Magna Carta was the first step toward constitutional, or limited, government. In the centuries that followed, monarchs continued to claim absolute power. But those who challenged the monarch's power

EATON RAPIDS
HIGH SCHOOL LIBRARY

would cite the Magna Carta as the historic and legal basis for their arguments.

## PARLIAMENT EVOLVES

Over centuries, the Great Council formed by William the Conqueror developed into a two-chamber, or bicameral, body. One chamber, the House of Lords, included nobles who inherited their seats and privileges. The other chamber, the House of Commons, was made up of commoners, who first were appointed, and later elected, to their seats.

Eventually the Great Council became known as Parliament. It served as an institution through which the monarch could consult with nobles, land owners, and townspeople. In other words, the role of Parliament was consultative. But gradually, over centuries, the people came to believe that Parliament should play more than a consultative role, that it should participate in making decisions and laws. Even so, the English kings clung to the notions of absolute power and divine right.

During the reign of the Tudors, the English monarchy reached its period of greatest power and brilliance. In 1534, Henry VIII broke with Rome and the pope over the issue of divorce, declaring himself the head of the Church of England. In the reign of Elizabeth I, in 1588, England defeated the Spanish Armada, becoming the leading world power. The English economy flourished through trade and piracy. English culture achieved a vitality and greatness personified in the poet and playwright William Shakespeare. But the power and authority of the English monarchy receded under the Stuart kings, who followed Elizabeth I, the last Tudor, in 1603.

## KING VERSUS PARLIAMENT

Henry VIII and Elizabeth I had wielded virtually absolute power. Yet by and large, the Tudors had dealt with opposition through shrewd politics rather than arrogant threats and force. The Stuarts, by contrast, antagonized Parliament with their bold claims of absolute power. To those who challenged those claims, the Stuart king James I replied, "It is atheism and blasphemy to dispute what God can do."

Among other rights, the Stuarts claimed the right to conduct foreign policy without the advice or consent of Parliament. They claimed the right to wage unpopular wars and to finance them in ways Parliament considered illegal—by borrowing money from foreign countries, for example. Eventually the struggle between king and Parliament led to civil war, which ended with the defeat of Charles I and his execution by the army in 1649.

In place of the monarchy, the army established a republic headed by the Puritan general Oliver Cromwell. Cromwell's republic, however, deteriorated into a military dictatorship. His efforts to reestablish a parliamentary form of government ran afoul of the stubborn fact that most Englishmen rejected Cromwell's Puritanism and longed for the reestablishment of the monarchy. When Cromwell died in 1658, Parliament restored the monarchy under Charles II, another Stuart.

The old conflict between king and Parliament was soon rekindled, but did not reach its climax until the reign of James II, who assumed the throne in 1685. Protestants feared that James, a Roman Catholic, might force his country into a religious reunion with Rome and the pope. Again there was the threat of civil war. By 1688, James was in flight to France, having thrown the Great Seal of the Kingdom into the Thames.

On January 28, 1689, the House of Commons declared the throne of England vacant and offered the crown to William and Mary of Orange, Protestant relatives of the Stuarts. William and Mary accepted the crown, agreeing to respect the "true, ancient, and indubitable rights of the people of this realm." John Locke himself approved, condemning the Stuart monarchs for breaking the social contract between rulers and the people.

So ended the Glorious Revolution of 1688–89. Parliament had secured its existence and its rights as an indispensable partner in governing. But it was by no means the dominant partner. The king was still the active head of government, and its ministers were responsible to him.

In the years that followed, Parliament greatly expanded its powers. No bill could become law unless passed by both houses and signed by the king. And after 1714 no king withheld assent from a bill approved by Parliament.

Later in the 1700s, the king began to select his ministers— the heads of government departments—from persons who had the confidence and support of a majority in the House of Commons. As this practice became customary, a new belief became established—the belief that ministers of government are responsible and accountable not to the king, but to Parliament.

## THE STRUGGLE FOR DEMOCRACY

By the early nineteenth century, Parliament possessed the full powers of government. But in those years the House of Commons was far from being a representative body. Only one-fifth of its members were popularly elected, and only property owners could vote. The unpropertied majority and religious dissenters had no representation at all. The next phase in the development of the British system was the struggle to make Parliament more democratic.

The great landmark in the democratization of the British system was the Reform Act of 1832. It created more election districts in new and growing cities. It eliminated many of the "rotten boroughs," which were districts with more representatives than their population entitled them to. These reforms increased the number of eligible voters from half a million to three-fourths of a million, allowing many members of the growing middle class to vote for the first time.

Two later reform acts extended the franchise, or right to vote, to skilled workers and farmers, and eliminated property qualifications for voting. By 1884 nearly every male over the age of twenty had the right to vote. With the enfranchisement of women in 1918, almost all of the population over the age of twenty could vote. In 1970 the voting age was reduced to eighteen.

The century-long movement to extend the franchise changed the British system in three important ways. It made political parties more important, causing them to become better organized and disciplined. It made the House of Commons truly representative of the people, causing it to become more important and powerful than the House of Lords. Gradually, the powers of the Lords were whittled away to the power to delay nonfinancial bills for one year. All of these changes tended to undermine the power of the monarch, so that by the twentieth century the king was reduced to no more than a figurehead.

## THE BRITISH SYSTEM TODAY

Despite Britain's long history of government by law, or constitutionalism, the British constitution has never been set down in a single document. It is formed partly by such documents as the Magna Carta, partly by acts of Parliament, partly by court decisions, common law, and tradition. The British have not found it necessary to put their constitution in writing because their political culture includes a broad consensus on the basic questions of power. Most of the British agree on who should rule, on what the limits of power and the rights of individuals should be, and on the general purposes of power. This consensus has been the source of great stability.

According to the rules of the unwritten constitution, the monarch—presently a queen—is the official head of the state—the United Kingdom of Great Britain and Northern Ireland. But the queen does not head the government which directs the affairs of state. She has only the right to "be consulted, to encourage, and to warn."

The "Queen's Government" is a parliamentary system led by a prime minister. A parliamentary system is characterized by a fusion of executive, legislative, and judical powers quite unlike the separation of powers in the American system. The British Parliament is the supreme law-making body, or legislature, in the United Kingdom. It is the supreme executive body of government as well, carrying out and enforcing the laws that it makes. And it is what Americans would call a "supreme court," with the power to decide conflicts over the meaning of laws. No court or other authority can override an act of Parliament.

The United Kingdom is a unitary state. In a unitary state all power flows from the center. All local governments derive their power from the national government. Parliament is supreme over every local government in England, Scotland, Wales, and Northern Ireland. Local governments and the laws they make could be abolished at Parliament's will.

The Americans who wrote the U.S. Constitution saw the parlimentary fusion of powers as an invitation to the concentration of power and tyranny. In theory, Parliament could assert absolute power; in practice, it has not done so. The House of Commons does not interfere with the day-by-day actions of the officials, the civil servants, the bureaucrats, or the judges it appoints. The tenure of judges is guaranteed during "good behavior," giving them immunity from political pressures.

## FORMING A GOVERNMENT

Members of the House of Commons are elected for a maximum term of five years. In a parliamentary system some of the legislators are called on to "form a government"—that is, to put together what Americans would call the executive branch of government. By tradition it is the leader of the party that wins a majority of seats in the House of Commons whom the queen asks to become prime minister. The prime minister then nominates for the queen's formal approval the entire ministerial team—the hundred or so men and women who will run the executive branch of the government. Ministers must hold seats either in the House of Commons or the House of Lords, so that they can be held accountable to their parties and the voters.

The prime minister also appoints some of the ministers to his or her cabinet. The cabinet is a small group of from sixteen to twenty-three persons who form a steering committee of Parliament. It is the cabinet that decides what matters Parliament will consider, and when.

The law requires that elections to Parliament be held at least every five years, but a prime minister may ask and receive "permission" from the queen to dissolve Parliament before its five-year term has ended. In this way, a prime minister can seize a favorable opportunity to run for reelection and gain a greater majority in Parliament. If a prime minister resigns as party leader, his or her successor becomes the new prime minister.

The British political system is a two-party system. Only twice have enough people voted for minor parties to deprive one of the two major parties of an absolute majority in Parliament. British parties are highly disciplined. Candidates of the major parties are chosen by their parties, not by the voters. Candidates must agree to support their party's platform and, once elected, to vote as they are instructed by party leaders. Voting with the opposition party is almost unknown; abstentions from voting with one's party are uncommon.

In Britain's two-party system, the party that loses the general election is known as the opposition party. The opposition enjoys special privileges in Parliament. Members of the opposition have the right to question the prime minister in the House of Commons. Because it controls the second largest number of votes in Commons, the opposition can sometimes block the majority party by joining forces with lesser parties. Finally, the opposition can call for a parliamentary "vote of confidence" on a decision by the majority party. If the ruling party should lose the vote of confidence, the government must resign, and new elections are held.

## POLITICAL PARTIES
## AND INTEREST GROUPS

The two major parties in Britain today are the Conservative Party, whose members are known as Tories, and the Labor Party, the Laborites, who are socialists. The Conservatives appeal largely to the middle and upper-middle classes, but receive support from some working-class and poor people as well. The Conservative program emphasizes private ownership, less government interference in the economy, and the encouragement of private initiative throughout society.

As socialists, the Laborites have traditionally followed a nonviolent, less extreme path than Marxist socialists, such as the Russian Communists. The party does contain a Marxist wing, however. The Labor Party's chief support comes from organized labor and the very poor, and from many intellectuals and other groups as well. Laborites advocate public ownership of basic industries, policies that will promote a more equal distribution of wealth, and a greater emphasis on social welfare—better opportunities and rewards for workers, for example.

Interest groups are another vital part of the British political system. British history has encouraged their growth and independence. They work effectively to advance the interests of their members—ethnic and nationalist groups, workers, farmers, manufacturers, and other powerful groups throughout British society.

## AN OVERVIEW

The earliest lasting influence on British political culture was the Roman system of justice. From Roman justice came the belief in equality before the law. This belief became ingrained in British political culture, developing into the concept of constitutionalism, or government limited by law. Later, other widely shared beliefs—such as the belief in representative government and majority rule—reinforced the developing democratic system.

Another very important influence on the British system was the development of a monarchy strong enough to unify and centralize the country, but not strong enough to oppress it. The noble landlords, and later the rising middle classes and the workers, became powerful enough to challenge the king, asserting their own rights and privileges. These groups were able to balance the power of the monarch and prevent the rise of absolute government.

The belief in equal justice, representative government, and majority rule, as well as the existence of independent and powerful groups, led to the evolution of Parliament. In Parliament different groups could assert and claim their right to representation. Different groups gained experience in self-government, developing the parliamentary procedures that enabled them to work together. Early in their history the British agreed on how to disagree.

# 5

## The United States:
## The Great Compromisers

*I go for honorable compromise wherever
it can be made. Life itself is but a
compromise between death and life,
the struggle continuing throughout
our whole existence until the great
destroyer finally triumphs. . . . Let
no one who is not above the frailties of
our common nature disdain compromise.*

*Henry Clay,
"the Great Compromiser," 1850*

In 1831 a young Frenchman, Alexis de Tocqueville, landed in Newport, Rhode Island, to begin a nine-month tour across the twenty-four states that then made up the United States of America. The book he wrote on his return to France has shaped the world's perception of American society. Even today de Tocqueville's *Democracy in America* offers insights on American democracy as profound and provocative as when they were written.

The new nation was mostly middle class, with no aristocracy. De Tocqueville wrote, "No novelty . . . struck me more vividly than the equality of conditions." No matter where Americans lived or what they did, de Tocqueville claimed, they considered themselves as good as anyone else.

This shared belief in equality represented a radical break with history, said de Tocqueville. It was the basis of a new political culture. Elsewhere, people accepted the social position, however inferior, that they had inherited. They accepted the privilege that others enjoyed simply by virtue of birth. But not the Americans. What de Tocqueville described as the "never dying, ever kindling hatred . . . against the smallest privilege" was the heart of a developing democratic culture.

## JOURNEY INTO THE WILDERNESS

The foundations of an American political culture go back at least two centuries before de Tocqueville, to the Pilgrims' "errand into the wilderness" to gain religious freedom. The Pilgrims' ship, the *Mayflower*, arrived off Cape Cod in November 1620 after a long and dangerous crossing. But before landing in a wilderness where there was no supreme power—no king, no courts, no sheriff—they drew up a kind of constitution, the Mayflower Compact. In this document they agreed to make laws for the good of the colony as a whole. They further agreed that all males over the age of twenty would participate in making decisions. The Mayflower Compact was the earliest expression in the colonies of government based on the consent of the governed.

Wherever they lived, most American colonists thought of themselves as British citizens, with all the traditional rights of British citizens. The colonists bought clothing and manufactured goods from Britain. They read British books and newspapers. They looked to Great Britain for protection against the Indians and the French, who claimed much of North America west of the Appalachian Mountains. Beyond insisting that the colonies do most of their trading with Britain, London seemed content to leave the colonists alone.

But that attitude changed in 1763, when Great Britain won most of France's territory in North America—lands that stretched from the Appalachians to the Mississippi River. From a narrow, coastal strip, the colonies expanded overnight into a great empire. The opportunities for homesteaders, traders, trappers, and others were staggering.

But Britain had other plans for the newly won lands. Parliament enacted laws forbidding the colonists from developing the new territories. At the same time, Parliament enacted stringent new taxes to pay for the costly war with France and to administer the new territories.

## AMERICAN NATIONALISM

There were many colonists who hoped to get rid of the oppressive taxes and remain British. Yet even these "loyalists" agreed with the patriots that Parliament was guilty of "taxation without representation."

As British subjects, the colonists shared the belief that they ought to be represented in decisions that affected them. It was this widely shared belief in representation that cemented the opposition to Great Britain.

In 1774, when Patrick Henry told the Continental Congress, "I am not a Virginian, but an American," he expressed a new and growing spirit of American nationalism, a belief that the colonies had acquired their own identity.

By 1776, when representatives of the thirteen colonies met in the Continental Congress in Philadelphia, a consensus had taken shape. Thomas Jefferson expressed that consensus in the Declaration of Independence, which was signed by the representatives to the Congress on July 4:

The history of the present King of Great Britain is a history of repeated injuries and usurpations, all having in direct object the establishment of an absolute Tyranny over these States. . . .

In every stage of these Oppressions We have Petitioned for Redress in the most humble terms: Our repeated Petitions have been answered only by repeated injury. A Prince whose character is thus marked by every act which may define a Tyrant, is unfit to be the ruler of a free People. . . .

We, therefore, the Representatives of the United States of America . . . do, in the Name, and by Authority of the good People of these Colonies, solemnly publish and declare, That these United Colonies are, and of Right ought to be Free and Independent States. . . .

## THE CRITICAL PERIOD

In 1776 each of the American colonies became a sovereign state—an independent country with final authority over its people. When the colonists defeated Britain in 1781, their victory gave the ideas and experience of the Americans worldwide influence, but victory did not lead to political union. Most Americans agreed that some form of central government was essential to coordinate policies that affected all thirteen states—foreign policy, for example.

Most of the Americans shared a common Britain parliamentary background, including a respect for traditional legal and political procedures. They shared a belief in natural rights, limited and representative government, and a fear of absolute power. But the Americans were divided by issues and interests. Property owners, merchants, and city dwellers felt a real need for the protection offered by government. Farmers and settlers on the frontier doubted whether they needed a government at all.

The societies of North and South stood in marked contrast to one another. The economies of North, South, and West rested on different foundations. Within each region there were strong rivalries. What kind of government could satisfy the conflicting needs and goals of so many regions and groups?

In 1777 the Continental Congress approved the first U.S. constitution; it was called the Articles of Confederation. Under the Articles, each state kept "its sovereignty, freedom, and independence." The newly created national government consisted of only one branch, Congress. Each state had one vote in Congress, which could declare war, make peace, and make treaties of commerce. But Congress could not collect taxes, regulate trade among the states, force any state to cooperate with any other, or tell a state how to deal with its own citizens.

So began what historians call "the critical period" in the history of the new American republic. Without revenue, the new national government had to beg states for money to pay the Army. Without the power to regulate trade between and among states, it was powerless to stop the quarrels that broke out among states over commerical dealings.

There was talk of civil war, and some believed that the new nation was doomed. But others saw a stronger national government as the solution, and in 1787, twelve of the thirteen states sent representatives to a Constitutional Convention to change and strengthen the Articles of Confederation. They did much more than that.

## THE END OF THE
## FIRST U.S. GOVERNMENT

George Washington was chosen to preside over the Constitutional Convention. Among the forty-five delegates were merchants, planters, and soldiers. More than half were lawyers or government officials familiar with the law. After their initial discussions, the delegates agreed that the government created by the Articles of Confederation never could work. A new and stronger national government was a matter of survival for all the states.

The new government, the delegates believed, would need the power to tax, to regulate trade among the states, and to raise armies. It would have to be powerful enough to defend the states, but not powerful enough to threaten their rightful powers or the rights of individuals.

But philosophical agreement alone could not bridge the conflicts among the delegates. Strong skills in compromise were decisive. Despite bitter differences and threats to leave the Convention, the delegates debated through the summer of 1787. By the end of summer, they had agreed on a draft of the U.S. Constitution.

## A BUNDLE OF COMPROMISES

Through a series of brilliant compromises, those who drafted the U.S. Constitution managed to resolve every serious conflict, whether political, economic, or philosophical. A conflict between small and large states was resolved through the Connecticut Compromise. This provided for a bicameral Congress consisting of a Senate in which each state is equally represented, and a House of Representatives in which the states are represented in proportion to their population.

There were deeper conflicts than this, and more ingenious compromises. Most of the delegates favored a stronger government than that created by the Articles of Confederation. But many delegates feared that a strong national government would trample on the powers of the states and the rights of individuals. Some of the delegates were more aristocratic than democratic, favoring government by the few. Other delegates were strongly democratic, seeing no cause to fear the people. Still others feared that if the people were given too great a role in the new government, they could vote a dictator into power. The Constitution resolved these conflicting fears and expectations through the adoption of three principles.

First it created a federal system, granting some powers to the national, or federal, government, but reserving others to the state governments. In the American federal system, the rights and powers of the states come from the Constitution, just as those of the federal government do. The federal government has often differed with state governments on the limits of state and federal power. But the federal government cannot abridge any right which the Constitution clearly gives the states—the right to administer education and schools, for example.

To prevent the federal government from becoming too strong, the Constitution purposely weakens it, dividing the powers of government among three independent branches. These are the presidency, or executive branch; the Congress, or legislative branch; and the courts, which are the judicial branch of government. This arrangement is called the separation of powers.

To prevent the concentration of power in any one branch of government, the Constitution gives each branch the power to check the powers of the other two branches. The president can veto laws passed by Congress. With sufficient votes, Congress can override a veto by the president. The Senate must approve key presidential appointments, as well as declarations of war. The House can bring charges against, or impeach, a president, judge, or federal official. The Supreme Court can strike down a law that both Congress and the president have approved by declaring it unconstitutional. This constitutional principle is called checks-and-balances.

All three principles—federalism, the separation of powers, and checks-and-balances—are safeguards against the accumulation of power by one person, party, or group. All three principles represent major compromises between those who favored a strong federal government and those who feared it, between those who feared the people and those who championed them. To control the new federal government completely, it would be necessary to win control of the House of Representatives, the Senate, and the presidency—all of whose members are elected by different groups of people at different times for different terms.

The U.S. Constitution creates a republic that both aristocrats and the people would find difficult to subvert. As de Tocqueville described it, the Constitution is the greatest achievement of the Americans:

> All ages have furnished the spectacle of a people struggling with energy to win its independence. . . . But it is new in the history of society to see a great people turn a calm and scrutinizing eye upon itself when informed by the legislature that the wheels of its government are stopped, to see it carefully examine the extent of the evil, and patiently wait two whole years until a remedy is discovered, to which it voluntarily submitted without its costing a tear or a drop of blood from mankind.

> The assembly which accepted the task of composing the second Constitution was small; but George Washington was its president, and it contained the finest minds and noblest characters that had ever appeared in the New World.

—39

## THE LIVING CONSTITUTION

The U.S. Constitution has survived to become the world's oldest constitution largely because its framers left many blank spaces to be filled in by the future. It has developed in response to new conditions through the process of amendment, and through judicial review, a process which permits the Supreme Court to declare laws unconstitutional if they conflict with the Constitution.

Just as conflict between king and Parliament led to the evolution of the British system, so conflict over the interpretation of the Constitution has led to the development of the American system. In the mid-nineteenth century, Southerners and Northerners disagreed over the constitutional rights of the states. Slave states resented efforts by the federal government and Northerners to restrict the slave trade and abolish slavery. Moreover, the tariffs which had been imposed to protect Northern industry from British competition raised the cost of manufactured goods that Southerners bought. Early in the nineteenth century North and South were on a collision course.

The Northern, or Union, victory in the Civil War established the indissolubility of the Union: no state could secede from the United States of America. With the victory of the Union, slavery was abolished and black citizens were extended equal rights by the Thirteenth, Fourteenth, and Fifteenth Amendments to the Constitution.

But blacks were thwarted in their efforts to achieve equal rights—in education, employment, housing, and elsewhere. In the South an elaborate system of segregation was enacted through "Jim Crow" laws. These laws justified the separation of blacks and whites by requiring "separate but equal" public facilities—separate schools, separate hospitals, separate seating in public transportation, and so on.

In 1954 the Supreme Court declared the "separate but equal" doctrine unconstitutional. It ordered the states to desegregate their schools, and President Dwight Eisenhower sent units of the U.S. Army into the South to enforce the Court's order. Civil rights activists challenged the legality of Jim Crow laws through a strategy of nonviolent disobedience. As a result, hundreds of laws—local, state, and federal—were ultimately declared unconstitutional.

In the 1960s, the Supreme Court settled two other constitutional conflicts. In 1962 the Court ruled that representation in state legislatures did not reflect the principle of "one man, one vote" and was thus unconstitutional. The Court ordered the states to reapportion their election districts to ensure all voters equal representation. It also ordered that Congressional election districts be redrawn to reflect this same principle. The Court's ruling brought reform in some states where legislative boundaries had not been redrawn in forty to sixty years. Today, after each U.S. census, election districts must be made more or less equal through reapportionment.

In 1963 the Supreme Court ruled that no person accused of a felony can be deprived of the services of a lawyer because he or she is too poor to afford one. If a defendant cannot afford a lawyer, the government must provide one. Otherwise, a trial is unconstitutional. Like the Supreme Court's decisions on segregation and reapportionment, this decision contributed to the democratization of the American system. As a result of such decisions as these, the protection of the Bill of Rights has been extended to all citizens; political representation has become more equal; and justice is more easily available to all. Because the Constitution has evolved in response to changing social realities and demands, it is sometimes described as "the living Constitution."

## A PRESIDENTIAL SYSTEM

The American system is called a presidential system of government. In a presidential system, a president elected by the people is responsible to them, rather than to the legislature. Like the British prime minister, the president is the leader of his party. But the P.M. is responsible to his or her party and could be ousted as party leader. If that were to happen, his or her successor as party leader would become prime minister. Unlike the P.M., the president serves also as head of state, filling the role that the monarch plays in Britain.

As chief executive, the president is responsible for carrying out laws and administering the departments of government. The Constitution requires the Senate to approve the president's important political appointments. Like the P.M., the president has a cabinet whose members are the head of government departments. While members of the president's cabinet must be approved by the Senate, they do not sit in Congress and are answerable only to the president.

All laws require the approval of both houses of Congress and the president. That way the Senate and House can check one another, and the president may check Congress with his veto. No prime minister has veto power, for it would be meaningless. All bills that come from Parliament represent the wishes of the P.M. and the majority party, which the P.M. leads.

In a presidential system, the opposition party cannot call for a vote of confidence. The president and members of Congress ordinarily serve out their elected terms of office, regardless of how unpopular they or their policies may be. When different parties control the executive and legislative branches, important decisions may take years to reach. But a loss of efficiency was the price Americans were willing to pay for the separation of powers and checks-and-balances.

Like the British system, the American system is basically a two-party system. The two major parties in modern American politics have been the Republicans and the Democrats. Republicans have traditionally appealed to farmers, businesspeople, nonunionized labor, and suburbanites. The Democrats appeal largely to unionized labor, unskilled workers, ethnic minority groups, and city dwellers. Democrats favor a more active role for the federal government than Republicans do, particularly in the economy and in social welfare.

Interest groups play as important a role in American politics as parties do. Nowhere are they more numerous or active. Among the more powerful groups are those representing the interests of labor, business, industry, and agriculture. In Britain the centralization of power leads interest groups to focus their influence on the ministers of government. In the United States, where power is so broadly distributed, groups must try to influence state and national governments, and the executive branches of those governments as well as the legislatures.

As in Britain, there are traditional alliances between political parties and interest groups—between labor and the Democrats, for example, and between business and the Republicans. But no alliance of groups has proved strong enough to control the government all of the time. And the competition among them helps prevent the concentration of power in one group in government or society.

## AN OVERVIEW

English political ideas and procedures were part of the baggage the colonists carried with them to the New World. As colonists, they gained experience in self-government, serving as governors, legislators, judges, and administrators. With the British they shared a belief in law, liberty, and representative government. Being mostly middle class, with no aristocracy, they placed a higher value on equality.

They rejected the notion that, as colonists, they were in any way inferior. They believed they were entitled to the rights of British citizens, including the right to representation in government. They regarded taxation without representation as proof that British rule had become tyrannical.

The colonists' fear of abusive power was a decisive influence on the Constitution and the government it created. The division of power between the federal government and the states, and the separation of powers among three branches of the federal government are only two of the precautions they took against the concentration and abuse of power. The broad distribution of power in the American system encouraged and reinforced the growth of many independent, powerful, and competing groups.

Although they are largely middle class, the Americans are a mixture of many ethnic, religious, economic, and regional groups. Early in their history they discovered that self-government requires skills in compromise, and a practical and moderate approach to politics.

# 6

## *The Soviet Union: From Tsars to Commissars*

*I am your lord and my lord is the Tsar. The Tsar has a right to give me orders and I must obey. On my estate I am the Tsar, I am your god on earth, and I must be responsible for you to God in heaven. God cleanses the air with thunder and lightning, and in my village I shall cleanse with thunder and fire, whenever I think it necessary.*

*A Russian landowner to his serfs, 1847*

*When we Communists say "the state," the state is we—it is the advanced guard of the working class, the Communist Party of the Soviet Union.*

*V. I. Lenin, 1922*

*I cannot forecast to you the action of Russia. It is a riddle wrapped in a mystery inside an enigma.*

*Winston Churchill, 1939*

**T**he Union of Soviet Socialist Republics, or USSR, is the largest country in the world. Almost three times the size of the United States, it dominates not one continent, but two. It is sometimes called the Soviet Union, and sometimes Russia, which was its name until the Communist revolution of 1917, and is still the name of its dominant region.

The Soviet Union is the world's first communist state. In 1987 it will observe the seventieth anniversary of its founding by V. I. Lenin, who was also the founder and leader of Russia's Communist Party. Even today, ruled by commissars instead of tsars, Soviet society and government reflect values, beliefs, and practices that were established much earlier in Russian history.

The history of Russia began in the fifth century A.D., when tribes of Slavs moved into European Russia from the West. In the early ninth century, northern Russia was invaded by Scandinavian Vikings who were called Rus. It was they who gave Russia its name. Moving southward from the Baltic Sea to the Black Sea, the Rus gradually established their rule over the Slavs. In the 860s, during the reign of the Rus chieftain Riurik, Russia was a loose federation of city-states ruled from the city of Kiev. Each city had an assembly, or *veche*, in which all free male citizens voted on important decisions.

## WINDOW ON THE EAST

The difference between Eastern Europe and Western Europe is more than geographic. It is social, intellectual, and spiritual as well. In their earliest, formative years, England, France, and the other countries of Western Europe were occupied and influenced by Rome. The Roman influence is apparent even today in their languages, religions, and political cultures.

In its earliest, formative years, Russia was exposed not to Roman, or Western, influences, but to Byzantine, or Eastern, influences. Russia's Dnieper River proved to be the decisive connection with the Byzantine Empire and its capital, Constantinople. Once the eastern half of the Roman Empire, Byzantium became the center of the Empire and of Eastern Orthodox Christianity after Rome was invaded by barbarians in the fourth century.

Russians first appeared at Constantinople as raiders; they were repulsed. In 907, Russians led by Prince Oleg appeared once again in Constantinople, this time as traders. They succeeded in extracting rights of trade from the Byzantine emperor. These, in turn, led to closer economic and cultural contacts.

In the late 900s and early 1000s, Constantinople was the economic and artistic center of the Mediterranean world. In 970 an ambassador from Kiev to Constantinople wrote to his prince: "We knew not whether we were in heaven or on earth, for on earth there is no such splendor or such beauty, and we are at a loss how to describe it."

Trade and commerce with Constantinople brought new wealth, new ideas, and great changes in Russian culture. Among the most important of these changes were the adoption of a new alphabet derived from Greek, the adoption of Greek Orthodox Christianity, and the acceptance of new ideas about government.

## THE BYZANTINE AUTOCRAT

In Byzantium the emperor was regarded as the image of the "heavenly king." Official theory maintained that "as there is one God, so there is one king, crowned in the image of heavenly kingship." The emperor's power was both absolute and sacred: he ruled in partnership with God. Petitions to the emperor began with the statement, "Our souls have no duty but to look towards you, O Supreme Masters of the Universe." The emperor's role as agent and partner of God was symbolized by the great purple and gold double throne from which he transacted all official affairs. Half of the throne, empty to mortal eyes, was occupied by God Himself.

The emperor's power was absolute. He was above the law. He could regulate customs, which he supervised and reformed. He selected the clothing to be worn by his subjects. He possessed civil powers, making and unmaking laws. He nominated and appointed all officials, both civil and military. He was the supreme judge. He controlled the economy of the empire and personally administered its budgets. He exercised military powers, often leading armies in battle. And finally, he ruled the church as he ruled the state, making all important decisions himself.

Nothing in the Byzantine constitution balanced or modified the emperor's powers. There was a senate, which was nothing more than an assembly of high officials united in devotion to the emperor. The people were a mob to be fed and amused; despite efforts to tame it, it sometimes broke out in rioting and revolution.

There was a fatal flaw in Byzantium's system of autocratic government. Like Rome, Byzantium had no law of succession. In theory a man became emperor through election by the senate, the people, or the army, or by decree of the reigning emperor. But in practice, it was almost always through violence and assassination that emperors were made.

Only through force could imperial power be held in check. There was the force of arms, manifesting itself in military revolt. There was the force of aristocratic families—conspiracies and violence aimed at capturing the throne. And there was the force of the people exploding in riots. It was said of Byzantium, and later of Russia, that their governments were tyrannies restrained by assassination and revolution.

## ENTER THE MONGOLS

In 1237, Russia's connection with the Byzantine Empire was abruptly severed. In that year great armies of Mongols known as the Golden Horde swept across Russia and into Europe. The Mongol invasion dealt a fatal blow to Russia's Kievan culture and profoundly influenced Russia's political development. During the early stages of the conquest, and in later punitive expeditions, much of Russia was devastated. Democratic practices such as the city assemblies died out.

The Mongols occupied Russia for more than two centuries. Normally they were content to levy tributes and draft military contingents from among the Russian peasants. They left the Russian princes in nominal control of their city-states, although they meddled in Russia's internal politics, playing one princely family off against another and thereby perpetuating Russia's weakness.

In the late 1300s the power of the Mongols began to fade as Russian princes defeated them in open conflict on several occasions. During this period Moscow emerged as the most prominent of Russian cities, and it was a grand duke of Moscow, Ivan I, who defeated the Mongols decisively in 1480.

By this time, Constantinople had fallen, captured by the Turks in 1453. When Ivan married Zoe, the niece of the last Byzantine emperor, he established the claim of the Russian tsars to be successors of the Byzantine emperors and protectors of Orthodox Christianity. The religious advisers to the Russian tsars sought to preserve the Byzantine institutions, and to exploit the memory of Byzantine glory to their own advantage. One of these advisers wrote:

> All Christian empires are fallen and in their stead stands alone the empire of our ruler in accordance with the prophetical books. Two Romes have fallen, but the Third stands, and a Fourth there will not be. Thy kingdom, O pious Tsar, is the Third Rome.

And so the Byzantine conception of the autocrat was adopted by the Russian emperors. Ivan III took the title of tsar (meaning caesar) and autocrat, adopting the practices of the Byzantine court as well.

The half Byzantine, half Oriental tsarist government—served by a bureaucracy trained in Mongol financial and diplomatic techniques, and by the clergy, who developed the mythology of the Third Rome—needed only to eliminate its potential opponents to make its power complete.

## TSARS AGAINST THE PEOPLE

In Russia, as in England, there was conflict between the crown and the powerful landed nobility. In 1564, Tsar "Ivan IV, "the Terrible", withdrew from Moscow in the midst of a conflict with the *boyars*, or nobles. Historically, the boyars had played a consultative role in Russian government.

Ivan appealed to the people for support in his struggle against the boyars. Claiming to speak for the people, the metropolitan of Moscow, the head of the Orthodox Church, pleaded with Ivan to return. The support of the church tipped the balance in this conflict. Ivan returned and took a terrible revenge on his opponents. His army attacked the city of Novgorod, a center of opposition, destroying much of the city and executing and torturing thousands of its inhabitants. He killed so many of the boyar families that they were no longer an effective political force. In their place he established a new class of landowners wholly dependent on him.

It was Ivan the Terrible who launched Russia's policies of outward expansion, warring with Mongols in the Crimea, with Swedes, Poles, and Turks. In the next century there were wars with Persia, France, Poland, Sweden, and Turkey. Their overall effect was to strengthen the authoritarian nature of the Russian government.

In a constant state of emergency, the tsarist government could claim that representative government and civil liberties were luxuries that would make the government inefficient in its response to enemies and invaders. It could justify censorship and the suppression of free speech, free assembly, and all the other rights and freedoms which had long been established in Britain.

Serfdom was fastened on the Russian peasantry during these same years. To escape being conscripted for military service, many thousands of Russian peasants ran off to the newly conquered territories in Russia's southeast. Drastic measures were adopted to hold the peasants on the land. Finally, in the early seventeenth century, the peasants were reduced to serfdom, or virtual slavery. They were forbidden to leave the lands they tended for their owners. During the seventeenth and eighteenth centuries, there were great peasant revolts which were ruthlessly suppressed.

## WESTERN INFLUENCES

In the early eighteenth century, Russia looked westward, hoping to adopt methods and ideas that had made the major countries of Western Europe rich and mighty. As a young man, Peter the Great made an anonymous trip to Western Europe to study Western techniques himself. On his return, he made frantic efforts to build an army and navy as good as any in the world. In military affairs, Peter was successful. He defeated the Swedes and in 1721 secured a coastline on the Gulf of Finland. There he built a new city, St. Petersburg, which he made the capital of the Russian Empire.

Peter also laid the foundations for the industrialization of

Russia, but the Industrial Revolution was slow in developing. Even in the late 1800s, Russia was backward compared with Western Europe, and no sizable middle class had developed, as it had in Britain, France, Germany, and elsewhere.

But there was a growing number of factory workers who lived in misery in Moscow and St. Petersburg. There was no reform movement to address their conditions, as there was in Britain and in the United States. Instead their condition was addressed by a revolutionary party formed in 1903 under the leadership of V. I. Lenin. This was the Bolshevik Party, later the Communist Party of the Soviet Union, whose ideas and action program were largely influenced by the German socialist Karl Marx. Like the tsar's government itself, the revolutionaries adopted methods learned in the West.

In 1905 the workers emerged as one element in a movement demanding greater rights and freedoms. In response to these demands, the tsar created the Imperial Duma, or assembly, which was to be elected through limited franchise and to exercise only consultative powers. The Duma was too modest a concession, and the reform movement ended in a great general strike in 1905. The St. Petersburg workers formed the first soviet, or council, to direct the strike, which soon paralyzed the government. The tsar yielded.

In a proclamation called the October Manifesto, the tsar granted Russia a constitution. The new Duma would have real law-making powers, and the franchise would be extended to a larger number of people. But again the response was too little and too late. On December 22, 1905, "Bloody Sunday," there was severe street fighting and much bloodshed in St. Petersburg and elsewhere. There were punitive raids by the army to restore order in the provinces. Meanwhile, the tsar managed to float a huge loan in France and England so that when the Duma met he would not be dependent on the representatives of the people for funds.

On the very eve of the Duma's first meeting, in May 1906, the tsar announced the Fundamental Laws. These decided in advance many of the questions left open by the October Manifesto. The tsar was proclaimed autocrat, or supreme ruler, and retained complete control over the executive, the armed forces, and foreign policy. Changes in the Fundamental Laws could be made only with his consent.

## THE END OF
## THE RUSSIAN EMPIRE

No more of the history of the Russian tsars need be told. They claimed absolute power longer than any other kings, and they ruled longer than most. During their long history of authoritarian rule, a political culture took shape that would endure long after they had gone.

A belief in personal rights did not take root, for the government considered no activity purely personal. Instead of a tradition of representative government, a tradition of revolutionary violence developed. Deprived of a voice in government, some resorted to assassination and other forms of violence to express their disapproval and opposition.

Among those who believed that violence was essential for social change were the Bolsheviks. While they shared certain beliefs with other socialists—the belief that private property is a social evil, for example—they also believed that a small disciplined revolutionary party could seize power through violence and rule in the name of the workers. When the last tsar was overthrown in a popular revolution in 1917, it was the Bolsheviks who eventually emerged as masters of Russia.

## THE SOVIET SYSTEM TODAY

The Soviet Constitution creates a federal system consisting of fifteen "republics," which, for the most part, were nationality groups of the Russian Empire. These include Russians, Ukrainians, Armenians, Latvians, Georgians, and others. The Soviet system is neither a parliamentary system nor a presidential system, although it resembles both in superficial details.

The highest institution of the Soviet government is the Supreme Soviet, a two-chamber body whose term of office is four years. One chamber, the Soviet of the Union, is elected directly by the people. The other chamber, the Soviet of Nationalities, includes representatives of each of the republics.

The Supreme Soviet meets for only a few days each year. During its brief sessions, it elects the members of two smaller bodies—the Presidium of the Supreme Soviet and the Council of Ministers. The Presidium is a committee of about forty members, who exercise the powers of the Supreme Soviet. These powers are legislative, executive, and judicial. The Presidium

—52

makes laws, interprets laws, and appoints the ministers who carry them out.

The Council of Ministers, which is responsible to the Presidium, is the major executive body of the Soviet government. Its hundred or so members, or ministers, direct the departments of government. Its prime minister, or premier, is the head of the Soviet government. The Soviet premier has always been a leader of the Communist Party of the Soviet Union. For most of Soviet history, the premier has been the top party leader—the general secretary.

Because the Soviet system is a one-party system, the party and the government completely overlap. According to the Constitution, the party is the "core" of the government and of all other organizations in Soviet society. All power belongs to the party. Unlike parties in Britain and the United States, the Communist Party of the Soviet Union is an elite organization that not everyone may join. Its membership includes less than five percent of the Soviet population.

The party forms the Soviet government and controls all nominations for all high positions. In elections for members of the Supreme Soviet, voters are presented with one official party candidate. The popular vote is usually declared to be more than ninety-nine percent in favor of the official candidate. In electing members of the Presidium and the Council of Ministers, the Supreme Soviet always votes by acclamation to approve the party candidates. Never in the history of the Supreme Soviet has there been a single negative vote.

The competition for power takes place at the very top of the Communist Party in two small committees: the Secretariat and the Politburo. The Politburo is a policy-making body which defines the correct party position, or "line," on all issues in all sectors of Soviet society. The Secretariat has the crucial job of selecting key personnel in both the party and the government. The Secretariat also places, promotes, and removes officials in trade unions, industry, the press, the army, higher education, science, and culture—in brief, in every area of Soviet society.

The Secretariat of the Communist Party is the power center of the Soviet system. The leader of the Secretariat, the general secretary, is the top leader in the Soviet Union. In the Soviet system, decisions are made in the Politburo and the Secretariat and imposed on Soviet society by party-dominated organizations, including the government.

## AN OVERVIEW

Among the earliest influences on the Russian political system was the development of city assemblies in which all freemen had the right to vote. These were destroyed, however, during the Mongol Conquest. After the Mongols had been driven from Russia, the Byzantine Empire became the strongest influence on the development of Russia's political system.

From Byzantium the Russian tsars took the concept of autocracy, in which absolute power is concentrated in a single individual. Frequent wars and invasions gave the tsars a continuing justification for claiming absolute power. Authoritarianism became a tradition.

Although the boyars challenged the absolute power of the tsar, they were no match for his army and secret police. As a result, the one independent center of power that could have checked the tsar was broken. Other powerful groups—the church and the army—traditionally supported the tsar and his claim to absolute power.

In Russia, social reform could not be achieved through politics. No tolerance for conflicting views developed. Instead of a tradition of compromise, a tradition of violence developed. It was violence that brought Lenin and the Communist Party to power. As Russians, the Communists naturally shared many of the beliefs of Russian political culture. Tsarist authoritarianism has shaped the Soviet political system as much as Marx and Lenin have.

# 7

## Argentina:
## Generals and Caudillos

*Recognizing there is something
you do not know is an attitude not
usually found among Argentines.*

José Ortega y Gasset,
Spanish philosopher, 1933

*Without fanaticism, you
cannot accomplish anything.*

Eva Duarte Perón, 1950

*The most grave problem is
precisely that the people don't
believe in anything anymore.*

Deolindo F. Bittel,
leader of the
Peronist Party, 1982

**I**n 1515 the Spanish navigator Juan de Solis discovered the Rio de la Plata on the eastern coast of South America. Twenty years later the king of Spain sent Pedro de Mendoza to govern "the lands of the Rio de la Plata," and it was he who founded the city of Buenos Aires.

These lands were ruled first by the Spanish viceroy in Lima, Peru. Later they became part of the new Viceroyalty of Rio de la Plata, whose capital became Buenos Aires. The viceroys, who were appointed by the king of Spain, wielded almost absolute power, following the detailed instructions of the king. They issued laws and directed the economy and trade. They were responsible for enforcing even those laws that were harmful to the interests of the colonists.

All trade between Buenos Aires and Spain, for example, had to travel via Peru—across the Andes to Lima, up the Pacific coast, across the Isthmus of Panama, and then to Spain. A tradition of contraband trade that began then still flourishes today.

Worse yet, a disrespect for law developed, because government rules and regulations were so often harmful. A formula for evading the law developed—"I obey, but I do not comply." The Spanish colonists were left a tradition of inefficient administration and no experience in self-government. Argentine sociologist Juan Miguens describes the Spanish legacy as "an empty one, lacking the values and institutions upon which a healthy nation could be built."

## THE CAUDILLOS

In 1810 the populace of the Viceroyalty of Rio de la Plata rose against Spanish rule, and in 1816 they proclaimed their independence as the Republic of Argentina. What followed independence was nearly forty years of civil war and anarchy.

During this period of lawlessness, power passed into the hands of local *caudillos*, or leaders, who often led private armies. The caudillos rose and ruled through force of personality. They were daring, dashing, and macho. They attracted followers through displays of power and self-confidence. From the caudillos came the style of personalism, which is a quality common to all Latin American politics. In personalism a leader is not commonly chosen because he represents the political ideas of his followers, but because he possesses the inner qualities they most admire.

One reason for the rise of the caudillos was the existence of two incompatible societies in Argentina. There was the worldly Spanish and European society centered in Buenos Aires. And there was the lawless society of the pampa, or great plains, which were sparsely populated by gauchos—cowboys of mixed Spanish and Indian blood.

In political terms, the conflict between the townspeople and the gauchos was a conflict between Unitarios and Federales. The Unitarios favored a strong central government located in Buenos Aires. The Federales opposed the domination of the provinces by the capital and fought to retain provincial powers.

In 1829, in a gesture of compromise, the Unitarios of Buenos Aires invited Juan Manuel Rosas, a wealthy rancher and a Federal, to become Argentina's leader. Born on the pampa, Rosas had won the loyalty of gauchos and Indians. From 1835 to 1852 he ruled as a dictator. His spies and secret police intimidated and assassinated his enemies. His portrait was displayed on the altars of churches.

Through violence, Rosas advanced the unification of Argentina and the power of Buenos Aires over the provinces. He ruthlessly suppressed rebellions by provincial caudillos, ordering the leaders beheaded and their heads displayed in public.

In foreign policy, Rosas was equally ruthless but less effective. He made an unsuccessful attempt to conquer Paraguay, and for nine years laid siege to Montevideo, the capital of Uruguay, where many of his opponents had taken refuge. He quarreled with France, and the French fleet—later joined by the British—blockaded Buenos Aires, ruining foreign trade. Finally, a provincial caudillo led an army against Rosas, defeated him, and drove him into exile in England.

## THE UNITARIOS TRIUMPH

After Rosas, the townspeople produced a caudillo of their own, Domingo Faustino Sarmiento. During years of travel in the United States and Europe, Sarmiento had drawn up plans for reforming every sector of Argentine society. During the campaign against Rosas, Sarmiento had followed the army with a printing press in a cart, issuing bulletins denouncing the tyrant.

Elected president in 1868, Sarmiento sponsored a variety of social reforms. He encouraged the rapid extension of railways over the pampa, and the settlement of European immigrants. He sent troops into the interior to crush revolts by provincial caudillos. It was Sarmiento who finally established the supremacy of Buenos Aires, which in 1880 became the acknowledged capital of Argentina.

Even Sarmiento, who had always professed a belief in the rule of law, ruled Argentina through personalist methods. To bypass parliamentary opposition, he often suspended the constitution, governing by decree. He used his powers arbitrarily, sometimes to remove opponents from office.

Sarmiento's constructive work was continued by successive governments. So, too, were his personalist methods. It became normal practice for Argentine presidents to respect only such parts of the constitution as they found convenient. As a result, the presidency absorbed all the powers of government.

## NEW ARRIVALS, NEW FORCES

The opening up of Argentina's interior increased the need for immigrant labor, and the tide of newcomers rose rapidly. In 1895 the population of Argentina was less than four million. By 1914 the population had reached nearly fifteen million. More than fifty percent of the immigrants who arrived in this period were Italian, mostly from Italy's industrial north. Today they are Argentina's largest ethnic group, concentrated in the urban middle class as shopkeepers, factory workers, and bureaucrats. Farmers and ranchers, on the other hand, are mostly descendents of the Spanish, English, and Welsh.

Economic development created new political forces. Landowners amassed great fortunes and built mansions in Buenos Aires. Conditions for agricultural workers scarcely improved. With the growth of the urban middle class came demands for honest elections and representation in government. In the 1890s middle class elements formed Argentina's first opposition party, the Radical Party.

From 1880 to 1916, Argentina was ruled by a coalition of

conservative groups, including landowners and industrialists. It was these elites who chose the presidents of Argentina. Elections, when they occurred, were empty formalities. But a series of electoral reforms enabled the Argentines to choose their own government for the first time in 1916. Hipolito Irigoyen, the candidate of the Radical Party, was elected president with the support of both the middle class and the poor, who saw him as their champion.

Irigoyen introduced modest social reforms, such as minimum wages for workers. But he, too, meddled in the affairs of the congress and allowed massive corruption in his administration. Incapable of dealing with the problems of the Great Depression, he was overthrown in 1930 in the first of eight military coups in this century. In 1932 the military turned power over to the agricultural elite, and it was the landowners who chose Argentina's presidents during the next decade.

## THE RISE OF PERÓN

National pride drove a group of military officers to overthrow the conservative regime in 1943. They formed a junta, or group, which ruled as a military government. The military believed that the conservatives were out of step with the times. If Argentina were to become the colossus of the South, as the junta hoped, then it would have to modernize both government and society.

One officer, Colonel Juan Domingo Perón, clearly saw the need for a new type of caudillo. He must be the caudillo of the trade unions and industrialization. To win the support of the neglected masses, he would have to improve their condition. And he would have to be endowed with all the traditional qualities of the caudillo—masculine charm, style, and eloquence. Perón possessed all these qualities in abundance. And his friendship with a glamorous radio actress, Eva Duarte, had made him a popular celebrity.

In the military government of 1943, Perón chose a post that no one else wanted—the job of secretary of labor. He used his position to win the support of workers and unions. Eventually he was suspected of plotting for power and arrested by a clique within the military junta. In response to Perón's arrest, Eva Duarte effectively mobilized mass demonstrations by the unions. As a result, Perón was released, and his supporters formed a new political party, which nominated him as its candidate for president. In 1946, in the fairest elections in Argentine history, Perón was elected president, and the Peronist party swept congress.

Perón controlled the Army but derived most of his power from the support of the unions, whose leaders owed him their jobs. The rank and file owed him much, too, for Perón saw to it that they were well off, no matter what happened to Argentina's economy.

Perón encouraged the growth of industry by buying back control of companies owned by foreigners, and through large military expenditures. He used the high profits from the sale of Argentine commodities for industrial expansion. Though Perón badgered Argentine landowners politically and financially, he never tried to nationalize their great estates. But under Perón, Argentina crossed the dividing line between agricultural state and industrial state. When Perón was overthrown in 1955, the industrial elite was stronger than the agricultural elite.

It was the Army that overthrew Perón, promising to end the financial chaos his policies had created, as well as the corruption he had allowed and encouraged. He was succeeded by a number of civilian presidents chosen by the industrialists and approved by the Army. But in 1966 the Army seized power once more and ruled until 1973.

## AFTER PERÓN

In 1973 the Army bowed to popular pressures to allow Perón to return and run for office. President once more, he was unable to stop a bitter campaign of terrorism between the left and right wings of his followers. In 1974, as terrorism assumed the dimensions of civil war, Perón died. He was succeeded by his widow, the vice-president, Maria Estela (Isabel) Martinez de Perón. She ruled ineffectively until deposed by the Army in 1976. Most Argentines supported the coup, for it promised an end to terrorism and economic chaos.

Over the next two years the Army succeeded.in putting an end to terrorism, but only by adopting terrorist policies of its own. Since 1976 an estimated six to twenty thousand Argentines have "disappeared," victims of the military government and of local military and paramilitary organizations. In December 1982, fifteen hundred bodies were discovered in unmarked mass graves in and around Buenos Aires. The discovery heightened public suspicions that the junta is chiefly responsible for the mass disappearances.

In foreign and economic policy, the junta's record has been no more respectable. The Argentine economy has steadily deteriorated under military rule, and Argentina today has one of the largest foreign debts and highest rates of inflation in the world. As signs of public dissatisfaction mounted in the spring of 1982, the junta invaded the British crown colony of the Falkland Islands, located about 400 miles (640 km) off the coast of Argentina.

Because the Argentines have long regarded the islands as their own, the war was at first popularly supported. For a few weeks it seemed as if the Argentines had forgotten their troubled economy and "the disappeared." But when the Argentines suffered a humiliating defeat, the junta's support crumbled. There were public demonstrations against the junta and calls for its resignation. The leader of the junta was replaced by another general, but even this gesture did not appease the people, and protests continued. Finally the junta agreed to call elections in 1983 and return Argentina to civilian rule. With little experience in self-government and no tradition of constitutionalism, Argentina faces an uncertain future.

## THE ARGENTINE POLITICAL SYSTEM

Until 1949 the Constitution of Argentina was that of 1853, with modifications made in 1860, 1866, and 1898. In 1949 a new Constitution was drafted by the Perón government and passed by a constitutional convention. It gave the government far broader powers over the economy than earlier constitutions. In 1957, after Perón's fall, Argentina reverted to the 1853 Constitution as amended up to 1898.

The Constitution provides for the election of a president and vice-president by popular vote. Their term is set for six years, and the president is not to be immediately reelected. The president is to be commander in chief of the armed forces. He is given the power to make key appointments in the civil service and judiciary.

The National Congress consists of a Senate and a House of Representatives. The Senate includes two representatives each from Argentina's twenty-two provinces and the federal district of Buenos Aires. Senators are elected for a nine-year term. In the House, the provinces and the federal district are represented proportionally. Representatives are elected for four-year terms.

Argentina is a multi-party state, when political activity is permitted. There are at least fifteen political parties, not counting the Communists, who are outlawed. The Peronists are the largest party, although they are deeply divided. They include about a dozen factions, ranging from the extreme leftists who assassinated policemen in the mid-1970s, to the extreme rightists who assassinated the leftists. The Party's official head is former President Isabel Perón, who is in exile in Spain.

The Federal Party is a moderate party whose members hold beliefs similar to those of liberal Republicans in the United States. There is no party for Reagan-style conservatives. As a result, the military has filled the conservative role, usually allying itself with the agricultural and industrial elites.

In 1966 the leader of an Argentine junta declared that the constitution remained in force in so far as it was consistent with the junta's goals. This attitude has been characteristic throughout Argentina's history. Because there is no tradition of respect for the constitution, the constitution has little influence on government and no bearing on political reality.

Argentina is presently a unitary state. The governors of its provinces are appointed by the president and responsible to him or her. In other periods it has been organized as a federal state, with the provinces electing their own governors and controlling their internal affairs.

## AN OVERVIEW

The Spanish legacy of absolute and inefficient government was the earliest influence on the development of Argentina's political system. As colonists, the Argentines acquired no experience in self-government and few beliefs that would sustain self-government once they achieved their independence.

Instead, caudillos rose, who ruled through force. A tradition of personalism developed, in which leaders were admired not so much for their political ideas as for their personalities. With caudillos and personalism came the habit of not cooperating. For most of Argentina's history, caudillo has been against caudillo, the capital city against the provinces, the elites against the people.

No strong consensus on the basic questions of power developed. No tradition of limited government evolved. Military leaders continue to justify their coups by saying that their responsibility is not to the Constitution but to a higher idea they have of the nation. Other elites have other ideas of what the nation should be, putting themselves above the Constitution as well.

The Spaniards named Argentina the "land of silver." The society they founded in the sixteenth century is still based more on what an Argentine sociologist has called "myths and magic," than on law and compromise. Argentine novelist Jorge Luis Borges laments that the Argentine is "not a citizen, but an inhabitant," viewing his country as a land whose wealth can be endlessly exploited.

*People
and
Politics:
Four
Governments
in Action*

# 8

## *The Leadership Struggle*

*No man is good enough to govern
another man without that other's consent.*

*Abraham Lincoln, 1854*

*Supermen need no consent to govern;
it is their right, and theirs alone.*

*Adolf Hitler, 1923*

**W**ho should rule society? Who, in fact, does rule? The Soviet Communists claim that the working class rules Russia. In reality, the Communist Party rules absolutely on the grounds that workers are not yet fit to govern. In Argentina, the Constitution says that the people rule, while in reality the armed forces rule. In Britain and the United States, it is said that the people rule, yet some believe that powerful interest groups wield more than their rightful share of power.

One feature common to all political systems is the struggle for leadership. The way leaders are chosen reveals a great deal about a system, including who the participants in politics are, how representative the government is, and how democratic. Studying the leadership struggle is helpful in answering a basic question about a political system: Who rules?

## THE IRON LADY

In May 1979, Margaret Roberts Thatcher, the leader of Britain's Conservative Party, was driven to Buckingham Palace, where the queen of England requested her to form a new government. On the day before, Thatcher's party had won a comfortable majority in the House of Commons.

On accepting the queen's request, Thatcher became the "Queen's Prime Minister," and the head of Britain's government. That same day, she moved into the residence of Britain's prime ministers, 10 Downing Street, in London. Pausing on the doorstep to speak to supporters, she attributed her success to the virtues taught by her father, a small-town grocer. She said, "The things I learned in a small town are just the things that have won the election."

At Oxford University, Thatcher spent her days in a chemistry lab, and many of her evenings working for the Oxford Conservative Association, a debating society that elected her chairman in 1946. She graduated with honors in chemistry and worked for three years in a plastics factory.

At a conference of Tories in 1948, she was encouraged to try for the Conservative nomination for member of Parliament in Dartford, a heavily Laborite district near London. At the age of twenty-three, she beat out twenty-five others to win her party's nomination. But she lost the race, and lost in a second try the following year.

Over the next four years, she married, gave birth to twins, studied law, passed her bar exam, and began the practice of tax law. But she remained active in the party and kept an eye on politics. In 1959 she was elected to the House of Commons from a "safe" Conservative district in a suburb of North London.

In the 1960s she established her credentials as a tireless worker for Conservative causes. She became a popular speaker among Tory audiences, calling for tax cuts and attacking the "irresponsibly exercised" power of the unions. At one rally, she delighted audiences by quoting Sophocles: "Once a woman is made equal to a man, she becomes his superior."

She served as Minister of Education in the Conservative government of Edward Heath in 1970. In that position, she became controversial for her decision to abolish free milk for school-children. Her opponents chanted, "Mrs. Thatcher, milk snatcher!" Her children were jeered at in school. Deeply hurt, she was nevertheless strengthened through the experience. A biographer has written, "Iron entered her soul at that stage."

In 1975, while the Conservatives were out of power, Thatcher boldly challenged Edward Heath for leadership of the party. Through shrewd political maneuvering, she won the position on the second ballot taken by the party, before the overconfident Heath could rally. She moved to remodel the party in her own image.

## TRIUMPH

In 1979 the ruling Labor Party lost a vote of confidence in the House of Commons. In such cases, general elections must be called and a new government formed. Thatcher campaigned hard, promising voters no more than the bitter medicine needed to cure Britain's ailing and feeble economy.

She promised to cut government spending without touching such features of Britain's "welfare state" as socialized medicine, education, or pensions. She promised to "set the people free"

—*69*

from their government and to rebuild the economy on "the rock-hard and well-tested foundations of initiative and profit."

In the general elections, the Tories won 339 of the 635 seats in the House of Commons, a gain of 61. Labor won 268 seats, a loss of 51. To win as comfortable a margin as this, the Conservatives had to attract broad popular support, cutting across all classes and groups, including those who traditionally support Labor. One group that did not support Thatcher was Britain's small, mostly left-wing feminist movement. Undisturbed, Thatcher asked, "What's women's lib ever done for me?"

In selecting a woman as prime minister, the Conservative Party, and later the voters, broke with British tradition. But Thatcher fits the mold of Britain's prime ministers in most other respects. She rose through Conservative ranks as an effective and loyal worker. In the course of thirty years in politics, she gained the executive skills required to run the government. Equally important, she gained the parliamentary skills that are essential to a British P.M.—skills needed to lead the majority in the House of Commons, to outmaneuver the opposition party, and to quash all challenges to her leadership from within her own party. For unlike the American president, the British prime minister would have to resign if he or she lost the position of party leader.

In the British parliamentary system, candidates for party leader are chosen by their parties for proven skills in government and politics. Prime ministers are accountable to their parties and not directly to the voters. Yet the competition for power among strong and independent parties and groups, and their votes, give the people the last word in deciding who will rule.

## THE GREAT COMMUNICATOR

Once he was the most underestimated man in American politics— too old, it was said, and too conservative to become president. But in November 1980, after twelve years of trying, Ronald Reagan rode a tide of time-for-a-change conservatism into the White House, dealing President Jimmy Carter a stunning defeat.

Presidential candidates normally spend a career in politics, law, or government before winning their parties' nominations. They are normally lifelong Republicans or Democrats. Ronald Reagan is different. He began a career as a movie star in the

1930s. Only after that career faded did he turn to politics. He was originally a Democrat—"a bleeding-heart liberal," he says. His views began to change when he became strongly anticommunist in the 1940s, convinced that communists were trying to take over the movie industry under instructions from Moscow.

In 1952 he landed a job as host of the General Electric Theatre on TV and traveling lecturer at GE plants. It was in this period that he became a Republican. In his speeches he attacked government interference in industry and business. He began collecting examples of damage done by government interference with the free-enterprise system. His tours put him in touch with many conservative businessmen—potential supporters—in many parts of the country.

In 1964, Reagan burst upon the political scene with an impassioned TV appeal for funds for the presidential campaign of conservative Republican Barry Goldwater. The celebrity he had won as a conservative spokesman catapulted Reagan into politics and, in 1966, into the governorship of California.

## FALL AND RISE

He sought the Republican nomination for president in 1968, but the nomination went to Richard Nixon, who was renominated in 1972. In 1976, Reagan challenged incumbent Republican President Gerald Ford for the nomination. The primary battle against Reagan weakened Ford in his campaign for the presidency, and Ford was defeated by Jimmy Carter. Each time it was the more liberal Eastern Republican forces who defeated Reagan.

In 1976, Reagan believed that his chances for the nomination had passed. He was sixty-six years old, and no one had ever been elected president at that age. But friends prevailed on him to make one more try. He entered the Republican primaries once more in 1980, conducting an energetic and successful campaign that won him the nomination.

In the race against President Carter, Reagan campaigned on the conservative issues that he strongly believes in. He proposed an instant freeze on federal hiring, the quick introduction of three proposed ten percent income-tax cuts to stimulate the economy, and a budget-busting effort to restore America's defensive margin over the Soviet Union. He argued that the government bureaucracy stifles free enterprise and individual initiative. He promised to "get government off the backs of the people" by reducing the regulatory role of government and eliminating the departments of education and energy.

His victory cut across party lines and traditional loyalties, appealing to such traditional Democratic groups as labor and ethnic minorities. He did well in almost every income group and age group, and among both sexes. Only blacks and Hispanics, among traditional Democratic supporters, went strongly for Jimmy Carter.

In January 1981, Ronald Reagan became the fortieth president of the United States. Though he had been an office holder for only eight years, those years were spent as governor of California. Traditionally, governors acquire executive skills that the presidency requires. Unlike British prime ministers, the president does not lead his party in Congress, so legislative skills are less important.

Unlike the British P.M., a presidential candidate may come from "nowhere." Wendell Willkie, who was the Republican candidate for president in 1940, had been president of an electric utility. Ulysses S. Grant and Dwight Eisenhower had been military heroes. To win the presidential nomination, an individual must prove that he has popular appeal. He proves this quality in a series of state primaries. It is said that the major requirement for a president today is communication skills. If so, Ronald Reagan, called "the great communicator," is the prototype of the future.

## A GENERAL'S GENERAL

On April 2, 1982, Argentine military forces invaded and occupied the British crown colony of the Falkland Islands, which the Argentines had long claimed. In response to the invasion, Prime Minister Thatcher sent a task force to recapture the islands, 8,000 miles (12,900 km) distant from Britain.

After the Argentines were defeated by the British in June 1982, General Leopoldo Galtieri was forced to step down as president of Argentina and leader of the three-man junta that had ruled since it seized power in 1976. Though the decision to invade the Falklands had been a collective decision by the junta, which represented the Army, the Air Force and the Navy, it was General Galtieri who served as scapegoat.

In Argentina there is no agreed-upon method of succession to the presidency. One or two presidents have been popularly elected. Many have been elected in rigged elections. Most have been selected by elites—by leading members of the landowning or industrialist classes or the Army. Often the armed forces form a junta and rule as a military government.

Little is known of how a junta chooses a president. The choices take place behind closed doors, sometimes in barracks or private clubs, and sometimes in the presidential palace, as in the case of General Galtieri's successor. Reports of that meeting were leaked to the press, however, and these provide the scant information we possess on how a junta chooses a leader.

According to these reports, the junta's deliberations on Galtieri's successor turned into a shouting match, and finally, into a threat of force. The Air Force and Navy commanders argued that the Army had lost its credibility as leader after the Falklands defeat. They favored a civilian president chosen by the junta to lead the country until elections could be held.

The commander of the Army, General Nicolaides, insisted that the Army—as the largest of the armed services—was entitled to the presidency. His counterparts disagreed. Finally General Nicolaides threatened to put tanks on the streets of the capital to enforce his will. "I will crush you both!" he shouted to his colleagues.

The threat of force was decisive. Army General Reynaldo Bignone was chosen as president of Argentina, taking office on July 1, 1982. In a ceremony boycotted by the head of the Air Force and other military leaders, Bignone pledged to return Argentina to democratic rule by the end of his term, in 1983.

General Bignone's training and background are largely, but not exclusively, military. He entered the National Military Academy at the age of sixteen, graduating as a second lieutenant in 1947. He worked his way upward, becoming secretary-general of the army in the 1970s. In that post he often served as liaison between the military and the political parties, by then suspended.

For a country where civilian politics has been suspended more often than allowed, General Bignone's political experience is rather extensive. His political skills could be useful if the armed forces go ahead with their plan to return Argentina to civil government in 1983.

The lack of agreed-upon rules for selecting a president reflects the weak consensus of Argentine political culture. Not enough people agree on the rules to ensure that they will be consistently respected. And not enough people agree that abiding by rules is all that important. Even such noted champions of law and democracy as Jacobo Timmerman—a newspaper publisher who was arrested, tortured, and exiled by the junta—have supported military coups.

In the Argentine political system, force plays a more important role than law or tradition. Wealth also plays a most important role. The agricultural and industrial elites have influenced the choice of president much more often than have the middle working classes, who form a popular majority.

The history of Argentine politics has encouraged the growth of an authoritarian tradition in which the president is rarely the choice of the people. In Argentina, two or three elites govern in their own interests.

## THE MAN FROM THE KGB

The leadership struggle in Argentina is more often than not shrouded in mystery. By contrast with the Soviet way of choosing leaders, however, Argentina's method is an open book. In Argentina, it is always possible to say whose candidate a president is. He clearly represents the interests of one of three elites or, very infrequently, those of the people. But we do not know, and may never know, whose candidate Yuri Andropov was, or what coalition of groups enabled him to rise to top leadership in the Soviet Union.

Since 1979 or so, it was apparent that Andropov's predecessor, Leonid Brezhnev, was on his way out. Rumors circulated about his health, and at various times, he was reported to be suffering from cancer, heart disease, and a stroke. By 1981 it was clear that the struggle to succeed Brezhnev was under way and that Brezhnev's power was eroding.

In the Soviet system, the most important indicator of political strength is a leader's ability to promote his supporters to high party positions and to protect those already in place. By following the careers of secondary officials, Western observers are sometimes able to assess the strengths of top leaders.

In January 1982, Mikhail Suslov died. Suslov was a party veteran with immense prestige. He was a member of the Central Committee and a very important supporter of Brezhnev. After

Suslov's death, it was widely assumed that Konstantin Chernenko, Brezhnev's close aide for more than thirty years, would take Suslov's place. But instead sixty-eight-year-old Yuri Andropov, the former head of the secret police, or KGB, was named to replace Suslov. The move revealed that Brezhnev was losing control. And it made Andropov an instant contender for Brezhnev's post.

Yuri Andropov, whose father was a railway worker, was born in the northern Caucasus. As a young man he worked as a telegraph operator, film projectionist, and crew member on Volga riverboats before rising in the Young Communist League in the city of Yaroslavi.

After the Soviet Union gained territory from Finland in the 1939–1940 invasion, Andropov was sent to the new territory as head of its Young Communist League. During the German occupation, he organized guerrilla activities behind the lines. In 1951 he was brought to Moscow to be groomed for higher office. He joined the staff of the party secretariat. He became a diplomat and served from 1954 to 1957 as ambassador to Hungary, where he impressed his superiors by ruthlessly suppressing the anti-Soviet uprising of October 1956.

He returned to Moscow, joined the party Secretariat once more, and in 1962 became one of the party secretaries. In 1967 he was appointed head of the KGB, the Soviet intelligence and internal-security agency, where he remained for fifteen years. During those years, countless dissidents and critics ended up in psychiatric hospitals and labor camps.

Andropov left his post at the KGB in May 1982 to rejoin the party Secretariat, replacing Suslov. If there had been any doubts about his prominence in the party leadership, they were removed when Andropov was named chairman of the funeral commission for Leonid Brezhnev in November of that same year.

## WHOSE CHOICE IS HE?

On the day following Brezhnev's funeral, Andropov was named general secretary of the Communist Party. There had been no campaign, no rallies, and no opportunity for average Russians to make their choice known. But it is clear that Andropov had an election machine working for him long before the party made its choice.

No one knows precisely where Andropov's major support had come from. As former head of the KGB, he was thought to be a dark horse. The KGB summons up bad memories both for members of the party and ordinary Russian citizens. It was the KGB that had carried out the purges, executions, and mass exiles during Stalin's rule. Stalin's successor, Nikita Khrushchev, had ordered the head of the KGB under Stalin executed. In general, the party regarded the KGB as an instrument of control that could be turned against the leadership itself.

Andropov probably had the backing of the KGB in the leadership struggle, but observers do not know whether that support was decisive. There are signs that Andropov also had the support of the armed forces, and there were large numbers of troops around the Central Committee headquarters when his selection occurred. Like the KGB, the Army also has been viewed by the party as a center of power that has to be closely watched over.

Does Andropov's selection as general secretary mean that the Army or the KGB now has more power than the Communist Party? Or was Andropov the choice of the party elite as well? We do not know, and we may never know. Nor is it known what policies he will pursue. Many observers believe that his first order of business will be a crackdown on corruption throughout the party, and efforts to cut through bureaucratic red tape to make the economy more efficient and productive.

In the Soviet Union the competition for power takes place within the top circles of the Communist Party. Historically, the party has been dominant, although certain groups—not only the Army and the KGB, but the managerial class, as well—have exercised some influence on party decisions. To consolidate their power, party leaders frequently will appeal to these groups for support—by promising the Army more weapons, for example. Nikita Khrushchev said, "Politicians are the same everywhere—they promise to build bridges where there are no rivers." But in Soviet politics, promises are made to a narrow group of elites. There is no opposition party, so there is no broad-based competition for power. In the choice of leaders, the average Soviet citizen has no part to play other than to approve the decisions of the Communist Party.

## AN OVERVIEW

In the United Kingdom and the United States, the struggle for leadership involves competition among many independent groups, including political parties and interest groups. These groups may play a more important role in the two systems than the voters do. But the groups do, nevertheless, work to achieve the goals of their members, and almost everyone in Britain and the United States is represented by one or more of these groups.

Because the alliances among these groups are constantly shifting, no one group or alliance of groups is able to control the system, or the selection of leaders, consistently. By tradition, the Army and the churches do not play a role in politics. In Britain and the United States, more people participate in choosing leaders—and in politics, in general—than in the Soviet Union or Argentina. And it is the people who have the last word, because no candidate or policy can long survive without broad popular support.

In Argentina the leadership struggle takes place among a very small group of elites, with the people occasionally going against their wishes when given the chance to do so. The armed forces play the major role in the choice of leaders. In Russia the struggle for top leadership takes place among factions within the Communist Party. Historically, the party has dominated the Army and the KGB, but this dominance has recently been questioned. In the Soviet Union and Argentina, popular participation, either through elections or representation in interest groups, is minimal or nonexistent.

# 9

## *The Limits of Power*

*I am more and more convinced that
man is a dangerous creature; and
that power, whether vested in many
or a few, is ever grasping, and like
the grave, cries, "Give! Give!"*

*Abigail Adams, in
a letter to her husband,
John Adams, 1775*

**D**emocrats tend to disparage power, emphasizing its evils. Authoritarians exalt power, emphasizing its possibilities. Democratic systems define the boundaries of rulers' power in law. Law gives them the means of enforcing these limits. In authoritarian systems, rulers are given much discretionary power, and there are rarely ways of checking that power.

What should the limits on a ruler's power be? And how can rulers be checked when they overstep those limits?

## PARLIAMENT BEHEADS A KING

In England the struggle to limit the king's power reached its climax during the reign of Charles I. When Charles involved England in a war with both Spain and France, he went to Parliament for money and supplies. When Parliament refused supplies, Charles demanded loans from his subjects through methods Parliament considered illegal.

In 1628, Parliament reacted with a protest called the Petition of Right. Citing the Magna Carta, it reviewed the legal limitations of the powers of the English king, denying his right to tax, imprison, or punish anyone, or to quarter soldiers in the homes of private citizens, without legal authority. In reaction, Charles angrily dismissed the Parliament and for eleven years summoned no Parliament at all. He continued to raise money illegally.

In 1638, Charles tried to extend the Church of England to his other kingdom, Scotland, where Presbyterianism was the national religion. The Scots revolted, and the English draftees Charles had raised to fight them mutinied. With no money or trustworthy troops, Charles summoned a second Parliament. He soon dismissed it for being insubordinate. In 1640 he summoned a third Parliament, which met in a mood for conflict.

The new Parliament prosecuted the king's chief ministers, who had helped him to reign for so long without Parliament. It published another statement of its case against Charles. And it passed a bill requiring a meeting of Parliament at least once every three years, whether the king summoned it or not. The king,

—*80*

meanwhile, was plotting, seeking help in his struggle with Parliament from Catholic Irish and treasonable Scots. Both king and Parliament prepared for war, which began in 1642.

As head of the nation's army, the king could expect the support of the soldiers, but Parliament had greater resources. Success swayed from one side to the other, with the king holding Oxford, and Parliament holding London. Then Oliver Cromwell emerged among Parliament's commanders—a Puritan who had raised a small army and risen to the rank of general. Fired by religious enthusiasm, Cromwell and his "godly" regiment swept the king's forces before them and captured the king himself.

Parliament favored efforts at a settlement that would have left the king on his throne with limited powers. But when Parliament began to deal with the king, Cromwell and the Army intervened, turning out the supporters of the king from the House of Commons. The illegal body that remained—the "rump," as it was called—then put the king on trial.

The House of Lords rejected the legality of the trial, but the rump proclaimed "that the People are, under God, the origin of all just power," and that Commons has "the supreme power in this nation." The rump then proceeded with the trial, convicting the king as a "tyrant, traitor, murderer and enemy of his country."

Charles was found guilty and sentenced to death. One January morning in 1649 he was taken to a scaffold erected outside his own banqueting hall and beheaded. H. G. Wells has written:

> This was indeed a great and terrifying thing that Parliament had done. The like of it had never been heard of in the world before. Kings had killed each other times enough. . . . but that a section of the people should rise up, try its king solemnly and deliberately for disloyalty, mischief, and treachery, and condemn and kill him, sent horror through every court in Europe. . . . England, confused and conscience stricken at her own sacrilege, stood isolated before the world. . . .

## LIMITS MADE EXPLICIT

The conflict between king and Parliament was not finally resolved until the overthrow of James II, who—according to Wells—was "too dull to recognize the hidden limitation of the monarchy in Britain." When James fled to France, Parliament was careful not to give the Army a chance to intervene. It quickly moved to offer the crown to William and Mary of Orange, but only on condition that they sign a Bill of Rights promising to obey the "true, ancient, and indubitable rights of the people of this realm." Among the rights listed were these:

*That the making or suspending of laws without consent of Parliament is illegal;*

*That elections of members of Parliament must be free;*

*That Parliament should meet frequently;*

*That levying money without consent of Parliament is illegal;*

*That it is lawful to petition the sovereign;*

*That the maintenance of a standing Army without consent of Parliament is illegal;*

*That excessive bail never be demanded.*

On these conditions and others, William and Mary accepted the crown. Limits had been imposed on the British monarch once and for all.

## CHECKING A PRESIDENT

At about 2:30 a.m. on June 17, 1972, Washington, D.C., police entered the national headquarters of the Democratic Party in the Watergate office-apartment complex and caught five burglars attempting to bug the telephone of the party chairman. So began what Republican Senator Charles Percy called "the darkest scandal in American political history."

Over the next two years, newspaper, grand jury, and congressional investigations uncovered scores of illegal activities that could be traced back to sources in the White House or to the Committee for the Reelection of the President (CREEP). Formed to help reelect Richard Nixon, CREEP was headed by officials recently resigned from the Nixon cabinet and subcabinet.

In addition to the five burglars caught on the spot, two members of the White House staff were directly involved in the break-in. Top officials in the White House or at CREEP had inspired not only several other burglaries, but also the burning of incriminating evidence by the acting director of the Federal Bureau of Investigation; the use of FBI agitators to encourage anti–Vietnam War groups to violence, thereby discrediting the Democratic nominee, who opposed the war; plans to destroy the Brookings Institution, a center of criticism of Nixon's policies; and the compilation of a list of two hundred "enemies" targeted for character assassination or special harassment by the Internal Revenue Service. White House and CREEP officials had also accumulated illegal campaign funds by intimidating corporation executives and industrialists who did business with the government.

Some of these actions were illegal; all of them were unethical. Those charged with these actions argued that burglaries, spying, and the disregard of civil liberties could be justified by national security. Attorney General John Mitchell said that Nixon's reelection was necessary "to save the country."

By mid-1973, after a special Senate committee had exposed these and other actions, most Americans believed that the president himself was involved in a cover-up of the scandals. By October there were resolutions in the House of Representatives calling for his impeachment.

That same month, Nixon fired the special prosecutor for the Watergate case. The prosecutor had been promised total independence but ran into a brick wall when he tried to pry some secret tapes out of the White House. By the end of the year, the question was not whether Nixon would resign or be impeached, but when.

The combined weight of the charges against Nixon led to a formal impeachment inquiry by the House Judiciary Committee. The president refused to provide the committee with transcripts of Watergate-related conversations recorded in the White House. The Supreme Court then ruled that the president must comply. When the transcripts were released, they provided the evidence that the president had obstructed justice by directing the FBI away from the White House when its investigation led toward the president's staff. With the discovery of what was called "the smoking gun," Nixon's support in Congress vanished, even among Republicans. As it became likely that he would be impeached, he resigned, on August 9, 1974. Congress and the Supreme Court had checked presidential power, proving that the American system works.

—83

## THE IMPERIAL PRESIDENCY

Richard Nixon's defenders insist that other presidents have been guilty of unscrupulous acts and "dirty tricks." Other presidents have bugged conversations and harassed their enemies. Nixon's opponents argue that his offenses were more systematic and broad than anything known before. They emphasize that the central issue was the president's obstruction of justice, which violated his Constitutional oath of office.

But in a sense, Nixon was the victim of circumstances. The Watergate scandal took place within the context of an even more significant development which went back to the Great Depression and World War II. Since those years, presidents have assumed broader powers to deal with national emergencies. And in the 1970s, President Lyndon Johnson, and then President Nixon, claimed broader powers to wage war in Vietnam. Both Nixon and Johnson often chose to ignore Congress when Congress felt it had the right to be consulted on the conduct of the war. By the mid-1970s many observers in Congress and elsewhere feared that the office of chief executive had become "the imperial presidency." It was Nixon who bore the full brunt of those who sought to restrain the presidency.

Explaining Watergate to an English audience, historian Hugh Trevor-Roper drew a parallel with the conflict between king and Parliament in seventeenth-century England:

> The central issue then was royal power: the evident determination of the Crown to rule absolutely, and its evident success in building up the means of so doing. Those who opposed the king's aims, and disliked his ministers, saw well enough that unless they could halt this process, the whole system of English government might be permanently changed.

Trevor-Roper noted that supporters of President Nixon trivialize Watergate because they so much admire his foreign policy. Similarly, said Trevor-Roper, the foreign policy of Charles I was preferable to that of his critics:

> But the English thought first of their own liberties; and who shall say that they were wrong? So we should not measure the importance of the American Consti-

tutional crisis by the trivialities of Watergate, but should look at the struggle as a whole; a struggle which was already looming up, in vague, intangible form, before it was suddenly made real on this accidental battleground.

As a result of Watergate, the principle was re-affirmed that even the president is subject to the Constitution and laws as interpreted by the Supreme Court.

## THE SPEECH THAT SHOOK AN EMPIRE

In the Soviet Union there are no legal or other limitations on the power of the Communist Party and its top leader. Thus, between 1927 and 1953, Joseph Stalin was able to establish an absolute dictatorship unequaled in its violence. Stalin suppressed opponents through terror, perfecting a method known as the "purge." Purges were directed at those suspected of opposition to Stalin in the party, the army, the secret police, and every other sector of Soviet society. When a person was purged, he was generally charged with treason, tried, convicted, and executed or exiled. All of these acts violated the methods that Lenin had established.

Stalin's terror created deep fears in Russian society that interfered with the achievement of basic social objectives. High-ranking party members, government officials, and bureaucrats lived in fear for their lives. Where there is terror, there can be no stability. For Nikita Khrushchev, Stalin's successor, the challenge was to "de-Stalinize" the Soviet Union. By doing so, he hoped to lay the groundwork for a more rational, secure, and productive society, and to assure the party and the people that from now on, there were limits to violence as a method of rule. At the same time, Khrushchev hoped to discredit those who still admired the dictator and threatened Khrushchev's own power. In his memoirs, Khrushchev wrote:

> For three years we were unable to break with the past, unable to muster the courage to lift the curtain and see what had been hidden from us about the arrests, the trials, the arbitrary rule, the executions. . . . We did everything we could to shield Stalin, not yet fully

realizing that we were harboring a criminal, an assassin, a mass murderer! Not until 1956 did we set ourselves free from our subservience to Stalin.

## EXPOSING THE CULT OF PERSONALITY

At the Twentieth Congress of the Communist Party of the Soviet Union in February 1956, Khrushchev delivered a secret speech more than twenty thousand words long before a closed session of the delegates. In the speech he presented Stalin as a tyrant, a sadist, and an enemy of the party.

Khrushchev began by saying:

> It is impermissible and foreign to the spirit of Marxism-Leninism to elevate one person; to transform him into a superman possessing supernatural characteristics akin to those of a god. Such a belief about a man, and specifically about Stalin, was cultivated among us for many years.

Khrushchev revealed that Stalin had personally ordered the execution of party members. Of the 1,966 delegates who attended the Seventeenth Congress in 1934, 1,108 were later arrested or executed. Of the Central Committee elected by that Congress, seventy percent of its membership was arrested or executed within the next five years.

Unknown to the party rank and file, the Central Committee and Politburo had almost ceased to function during Stalin's last years. In those years, said Khrushchev, "Stalin became even more capricious, irritable and brutal; his suspicion grew. Everything was decided by him alone without any consideration for anyone or anything."

In denouncing Stalin's rule for its lawlessness and cruelty, and for its failure to respect party rules, Khrushchev had in fact given the party leaders a double pledge: that he would not use Stalinist methods against them, and that he would consult them according to principles established by Lenin. If the ideal of collective leadership could be reestablished, Khrushchev believed, no future Stalin could arise. There would be limits on what rulers could do.

Khrushchev's secret speech did away with the most horrible elements of Stalinism, but not with Soviet authoritarianism. When Khrushchev was removed from power in 1964, his removal was voted on by the Central Committee. In other words, the Leninist norms that Khrushchev extolled were the means of his removal. Under Stalin, he would have been shot or exiled. Instead he was allowed to live out his remaining years in peace.

Subtler forms of violence and terror exist in the Soviet Union today. But by revealing the crimes of Stalin in gruesome detail, Khrushchev did much to make party leaders aware of the possibilities for tyranny in the Soviet system. He reminded them of the need for vigilance and the merits of collective rule as an antidote to absolutism. Even so, with no tradition of limits or law, and no effective legal safeguards the Soviet system—like the tsarist system before it—is an open invitation to tyranny.

## SEARCHING FOR LIMITS IN ARGENTINA

In June 1982 a stunned Argentine nation learned of its defeat by the British in the battle for the Falklands. There were pictures of ten thousand Argentine prisoners whose return was delayed because the junta could not bring itself to say the war was over.

On June 15, the leader of the junta and president, General Leopoldo Galtieri, was scheduled to speak from the balcony of the presidential palace, as he had done several times during the brief war. But an angry mob of more than five thousand people shouting obscenities prevented Galtieri from making his appearance. Instead, riot police arrived, attacking demonstrators and reporters with clubs and tear gas. The generals had not merely lost the war; they had lost their grip on the country. Galtieri's successor as president and leader of the junta, General Reynaldo Bignone, promised a return to free elections in 1983.

The limits to the power of Argentina's leaders have so far escaped definition. Juan Perón was Argentina's most popular ruler, despite his gross disregard for constitutional limits. The military leaders who succeeded him are probably responsible for the death and disappearance of as many as twenty thousand Argentine citizens in "the dirty war" against urban terrorists between 1976 and 1979. In spite of the junta's disregard for human rights, there were no mass protests or calls for the government to step down. For the Argentines, thousands of disappearances were apparently an acceptable price to pay for internal peace.

But national humiliation in the Falklands was not acceptable, and popular discontent with the junta reached such pro-

—87

portions after the defeat that the junta decided to relinquish its power.

In Argentina, presidents and generals grab as much power as they can. There are no legal or traditional checks on rulers. When a civilian leader loses his credibility, the Army takes over. When the military loses its credibility, the mob takes to the streets, and the military retreats. When public dissatisfaction with civilian government grows, the military returns. The Argentine system, like the Soviet, is a system in search of limits; a system seeking to agree on limits.

What is happening in Argentina today will be decisive for the future development of Argentine politics. The junta is asking political parties to agree to certain conditions before they give up power. Among these conditions is an agreement by the political parties not to demand investigations into the disappearances, or trials for those responsible; not to investigate corruption in the armed forces; not to investigate the war for the Falklands; and not to investigate how Argentina's foreign debt rose from $7 billion in 1976 to $40 billion in 1982.

In effect, the armed forces are asking the civilians to accept that there are no enforceable legal limits on executive power. The leaders of Argentina's political parties argue that to grant the military immunity for its brutalities would further undermine respect for law and encourage further excesses by future presidents. If the civilians refuse to grant the generals' demand, take power, and then try those responsible for the crimes, an important precedent would be established. Limits on the power of the president could be made explicit. But if the civilians do not agree to the junta's conditions, the military is unlikely to return power to them. In its efforts to define the limits of power, Argentina faces the cruelest of dilemmas.

## AN OVERVIEW

In the United States and the United Kingdom, there is a tradition of constitutionalism, or rule by law, with rulers respecting limits on their powers or being held to account for disregarding them. In the Soviet Union and Argentina, there is no tradition of constitutionalism. There are limits to the power of rulers, but these limits are vague and changing and can often be backed up only through force.

In the British and American systems, formal and legal checks exist on the power of leaders. Special powers give the opposition party in Parliament a way of checking the prime minister and the ruling party. Federalism, the separation of powers, and checks-and-balances give Congress, the Supreme Court, and the states ways of checking the president and the executive branch of the federal government. Moreover, competing groups, especially political parties, have an interest in exposing and attacking abuses of power. This competition, along with a free press, helps to hold leaders accountable.

In the Soviet Union and Argentina, there are no formal or legal methods for checking the abuse of power—no opposition parties, no system of checks-and-balances, no independent courts and judges. Because free speech and freedom of the press are restricted or forbidden, leaders cannot be held to account by public opinion.

# 10

## The Rights of Individuals

*No freeman shall be taken, or imprisoned, outlawed, or exiled, or in any way harmed, nor will we go upon him nor will we send upon him, except by the legal judgment of his peers or by the law of the land. To none will we sell, to none deny or delay, right of justice.*

Magna Carta, signed by
King John in 1215

*The Fascist state organizes the nation, but leaves a sufficient margin of liberty to the individual, who is deprived of all useless and possibly harmful freedom, but retains what is essential. The deciding power in this question cannot be the individual, but the state alone.*

Benito Mussolini, 1933

In theory, most governments promise their citizens certain rights and freedoms. These include such personal freedoms as free speech, free assembly and freedom of belief, which define the scope of citizens' intellectual, political, and spiritual activities.

These promised rights and freedoms also include such civil rights as the right to vote and the right to equal opportunity in education, employment and housing—rights that shape the quality of human life. Finally, these promised rights sometimes include such procedural rights as the right of *habeas corpus*, which is a court order to an official having a person in his or her custody to produce the prisoner in court and explain the reasons for confinement. Procedural rights promote equality of justice, and give individuals a fair chance in conflicts with their government.

In practice, it is a different story. All governments are guilty at one time or another of violating individual rights and freedoms. Many governments violate their citizens rights systematically, mocking constitutional guarantees. The true quality of individual rights in any society can best be measured against the means open to citizens for correcting violations and abuses by their government.

## THE CIVIL RIGHTS MOVEMENT

Black Americans have been denied their rights for most of American history. They and other minorities have not yet fully realized the rights to which they are entitled. But methods exist through which abuses can be remedied. Some of these methods have been described in Chapter Five.

One method of correcting abuses is litigation, or going to court. Through litigation, thousands of laws discriminating against black Americans have been struck down. Another method for correcting abuses is legislation. By forming coalitions powerful enough to override segregationist forces in Congress, the civil rights movement of the 1960s was able to win passage of the

Civil Rights Acts of 1964 and 1965, and the Voting Rights Act of 1965. These acts were political breakthroughs.

Whether gains made by blacks in the 1960s will achieve broader reality is not known. Rights in any society are fragile, requiring constant defense. But the civil rights movement reveals that there are methods Americans can use to advance their rights and remedy injustice. The U.S. Constitution did not create a just state, but one that would work. If it worked, its framers believed, it could be improved. It could be used by minorities to achieve and expand justice and equality.

## RIGHTS IN THE SOVIET UNION

The Soviet Constitution defines the basic rights and duties of citizens. They have the right to work, the right to rest and leisure, the right to support in old age, sickness, disability, and so on. These rights are unqualified.

But freedom of speech, press, and assembly are granted "in conformity with the interests of the working people, and in order to strengthen the Socialist system." A prominent Soviet jurist has explained what this qualification means:

> Freedom of speech, of the press, of assembly, of meeting, of street parades and of demonstrations are the property of all citizens of the USSR, fully guaranteed by the state upon the single condition that they are used in accordance with the interests of the workers and to the end of strengthening the socialist social order. . . . In our state there can be no place for freedom of speech and so on for the foes of socialism.

Without these freedoms, there can be no opposition to the Communist Party in the Soviet Union. Democrats justify free speech on the grounds that the conflict of ideas leads ultimately to the truth. Russian authoritarians suppress free speech on the grounds that the Communist Party alone possesses the truth, which is embodied in the theories of Marx and Lenin.

One indicator of the condition of human rights in the Soviet Union is the annual report issued by Amnesty International, a group which won the Nobel Peace Prize for its efforts to win the release of nonviolent "prisoners of conscience" around the world. These are people who have been jailed simply for their beliefs.

In its 1981 report, Amnesty expressed concern for the harassment, imprisonment, and forcible confinement in mental institutions of people holding views disapproved of by Soviet authorities; for "frequent violations of internationally accepted standards for fair trial"; and for the harsh conditions of detention. The report points out specific rights that the Soviet government ignores:

> The authorities continued to convict prisoners of conscience for the nonviolent exercise of human rights— for "anti-Soviet agitation and propaganda, circulation of fabrications known to be false which defame the Soviet state," and for "violations of the laws on separation of church and state, and of church and school," which forbid teaching religion to children "in an organized way."

Among those who are prosecuted by Soviet authorities for their beliefs are Baptists, Seventh Day Adventists, Pentecostalists, and Russian Orthodox believers. Jews are prominent among the victims. Some figures suggest that nearly 400,000 of Russia's 1.8 million Jews would like to emigrate, as more than 250,000 Jews have done since 1965. But the government has cracked down, dismissing from their jobs thousands of those who have applied for exit visas. Being without work in the Soviet Union is a special hardship: because there is officially no unemployment, there is no unemployment insurance.

## THE HELSINKI MONITORS

One group of Soviet dissidents who suffered a fatal blow in 1982 was the Helsinki monitors. They were Soviet citizens who banded together in 1975, when the Soviet Union signed the Accords of the Helsinki Conference on Security and Cooperation in Europe.

At that time the monitors announced that they would observe Soviet compliance with the human rights provisions of the accords. Altogether, there were seventy-one members of the group. They lived in Moscow, the Ukraine, Lithuania, Armenia, Georgia, and other parts of the Soviet Union. Despite their small numbers they were threatening to the government because they included so many diverse elements—nationality groups, ethnic groups, religious groups, and workers. Moreover, they captured the attention of the world press.

As of December 1982 only eleven of the original seventy-one members have been spared official punishment. In its last statement, signed by sixteen monitors serving terms in labor camps, the group revealed that all the monitors in Armenia, Georgia, Lithuania, and the Ukraine had been jailed. The statement concluded: "In these circumstances, the group cannot fulfill the duties it assumed, and under the pressure of the authorities is obliged to terminate its work."

The dissident movement that began in Moscow in the mid-1960s was never a large one. Now it is decimated. The methods through which citizens fight for their rights are not available to citizens of the Soviet Union.

## MOTHERS OF
## THE PLAZA DE MAYO

When the Argentine armed forces deposed President Isabel Perón in 1976, their coup was supported by many, if not most, Argentines. It promised an end to incompetence, corruption, and widespread terrorism. Not all who died or disappeared in the junta's anti-terrorist campaign were terrorists, however. Most of them may have been nonviolent political activists or "liberals"—members of trade unions and church groups, for example.

In 1981, as part of its worldwide campaign against "disappearances," Amnesty International drew particular attention to the cases of sixty-seven missing children in Argentina. Some had disappeared with their parents after raids by the security forces. Others were born in captivity to women pregnant at the time of their abduction. Amnesty appealed to the authorities for information on their whereabouts.

In 1981 seven human rights organizations in Argentina for the first time held a joint demonstration in the Plaza de Mayo in Buenos Aires. They presented a petition to the government calling for "the reappearance, alive, of the disappeared prisoners." The police cordoned off the square and arrested some of the demonstrators. Two days later, General Galtieri, the leader of the junta, issued a statement denying that the government had any intention of issuing a list of disappeared persons. He stated that these cases were closed.

Amnesty International has condemned the junta for the arbitrary arrest and detention of persons without trial; for its "cruel, inhuman and degrading treatment" of political prisoners; and for failure to conform to internationally recognized standards for a fair trial. At the same time, Amnesty has identified sixty-eight hundred persons as "disappeared," reporting that it was not aware of "a single case in which an alleged abductor has been brought to justice by the authorities."

In 1982 a group of women who became known as "the mothers of the Plaza de Mayo," began picketing in Buenos Aires, demanding an accounting by the government for their missing sons and daughters. During the Falklands war they still marched, carrying banners that read, "The Malvinas [Falklands] belong to Argentina—so do the disappeared!"

## TERRORISM IN BRITAIN

Britain has had a terrorist problem off and on since 1916, when members of the Irish Republican Army sparked a revolt that led to the independence of southern Ireland. Today terrorists who call themselves "the Irish Republican Army—Provisional Wing" are waging a campaign to sever Northern Ireland from Britain, creating a united, independent Ireland.

The condition of captured IRA terrorists in Maze Prison in Northern Ireland has been a central concern of both Amnesty International and the European Commission of Human Rights. In August 1978 some of the prisoners submitted a complaint to the commission, alleging that the British government subjected them to "torture, and inhuman or degrading treatment or punishment."

The prisoners claimed that being required to wear a prison uniform and to work violated their right of freedom of belief and conscience. They insisted that they be recognized as political prisoners, not criminals, and treated accordingly.

After investigating the prisoners' complaints, the commission issued its report in June 1980. The commissioners had no doubt that the prisoners' conditions—especially those resulting from a "dirty protest" in which they smeared their walls with excreta—were inhuman and degrading, but self-imposed. The commission also found that the prisoners' punishment did not violate international conventions, and that the prisoners were not entitled to the status of political prisoners under national or international law.

Amnesty International notes, however, that "there have been alterations to almost every stage of the criminal justice process in Northern Ireland . . . and the overall effect of terrorism has been a weakening of the legal system, entailing a threat to fundamental rights."

For example, under the Prevention of Terrorism Act of 1976, a person can be held for forty-eight hours on the authority of the police alone. Higher officials can extend this period for another five days. Amnesty reports,

> Although these powers may only be applied to persons suspected of acts of terrorism, they have allegedly been used to detain people holding minority political opinions, or regarded as supporters of the aims (though not necessarily the means) of violent groups.

This finding confirms a recurring theme in government: governments are tempted to claim greater powers and threaten individual rights more severely in time of emergency.

The treatment of terrorists in the United Kingdom is indicative of British respect for equal justice and individual rights. The rights of those suspected of grave crimes are more often respected than not. As in the United States, legal and political guarantees exist by which abuses can be prevented and corrected.

## AN OVERVIEW

The British and American political systems rest on the assumptions that governments exist to protect individual rights, and that rulers and citizens alike are subject to the same laws. These assumptions have led both systems to spell out individual rights and devise ways of guaranteeing them. In both systems, independent courts and judges can reverse unfair and discriminatory decisions by the executive branch, by law-makers, by other courts, or by local governments.

Authoritarian systems rest on the assumption that all individual rights derive from the government. In both Russia and Argentina, rulers have historically been guilty of the grossest violations of individual rights and freedoms. In both countries, courts are subordinate to the wishes of top leaders and cannot overturn their decisions. In recent years the most important way of remedying rights violations in both countries has been the pressure of world opinion. Pressures by the United States, other countries, and international organizations have led both Russia and Argentina to release political prisoners, for example. But most abuses go uncorrected unless and until top leaders wish to correct them.

# 11

## The Goals of Policy

There never was a good war
or a bad peace.

Benjamin Franklin, 1773

Mankind has grown strong in
eternal struggles, and it will only
perish through eternal peace.

Adolf Hitler, 1930

**H**ow should governments use their power? What goals should they aim for? What policies should they adopt to gain their goals? All political systems, democratic and authoritarian alike, are occupied mainly in defining goals and devising policies to achieve them. But the way in which goals and policies are chosen reveals much about a political system, including the answer to the basic question of who rules.

## THE WELFARE STATE

In the twentieth century, a central concern of governments has been social welfare—better conditions for their citizens in education, health, employment, and retirement. Beginning with the Great Depression of the 1930s, popular pressures on democratic governments to adopt a more active role in society mounted. There was a need for government programs to promote the well-being of all who were threatened.

These demands went against the strain of individualism and free enterprise ingrained in the British and the American political cultures. But unlike the United States, Britain has a long tradition of socialism. In the late 1800s many distinguished figures declared themselves socialists and began advocating government ownership of basic industries, and a more equal distribution of wealth among the people. Ideas such as these made the British more receptive to the notion of a welfare state, which the Labor Party launched in 1945.

The first step in its creation was the nationalization of the Bank of England; the coal, electric, and gas utilities; inland transportation systems; the air transportation system; the iron and steel industries; and the telecommunications industry. Then the government moved to provide or expand a range of social services that gave the British "cradle to grave" security financed by compulsory insurance and contributions by employers.

These measures provide for income during sickness, disability, unemployment, maternity, widowhood, and old age. Special grants are provided for maternity and burial expenses. In short, almost every event in life is covered. These are insurance measures, but in a sense they aim to equalize social opportunities and rewards.

With the welfare state, Britain's government took a decisive step into spheres it had never before entered. But it was the people who favored the welfare state, and once it had been created, the Conservative Party, as well as Labor, respected its basic features.

## THE NEW DEAL

In the United States, as well as in Britain, the Great Depression and World War II had a profound effect on the role and goals of government. In March 1933, President Franklin D. Roosevelt asked the Congress for special powers to meet the crisis caused by the depression.

Roosevelt wanted special powers to implement his "new deal" programs. With a cooperative Congress, fifteen major bills became law within the first hundred days of Roosevelt's administration. These provided relief for the needy, help for ailing businesses, and corrections in the economic system.

Federal money was appropriated to hire people to build schools, post offices, sewage plants, dams, bridges, and hospitals. Thousands worked on construction projects sponsored by the newly created Works Progress Administration and the Public Works Administration.

For workers on relief, the federal government organized the Civilian Conservation Corps. For ten years, more than three million persons worked planting trees, building bridges, camps, and trails. The Agricultural Adjustment Administration paid farmers to produce less so that prices would rise and farmers could make a better profit.

In the 1930s the federal government thus began to play a more active role in American society. As in Britain, the government responded to the needs and wishes of the people. But in the 1980s, a more conservative view of the role of government was reasserted, bringing both Thatcher and Reagan to power. For both the British and the American systems, the challenge is to adjust the role and powers of government to the needs and wishes of each generation.

## WELFARE IN THE WORKERS' PARADISE

In the Soviet Union, the Communist Party and the government have always been the major forces in society and the economy. The government is the sole employer, the owner of all business and industry, the provider of all social services. While most Russians are assured of cradle-to-grave security, their standard of living has always taken second place to the modernization of Russia's backward economy and to huge arms expenditures.

After Stalin's death, Khrushchev promised the people more and better consumer goods. Once terror had been abandoned as an instrument of control, positive incentives had to take its place. In 1957, Khrushchev expressed the goal of catching up with the United States within a few years in the production of meat, butter, milk, and consumer goods.

The critical stumbling block preventing the achievement of these goals has been Soviet agriculture. Despite crash programs, no advances in productivity have been made in the past decade. Today Russians can scarcely feed themselves. Their condition is caused partly by the inefficient organization of agriculture into collective farms, partly by the discontent of peasants denied the profit of their labor, and partly by a low level of mechanization. But Communist leaders are not likely to consider other ways of organizing argriculture because collectivization is an essential means of control over the peasants. In the Soviet Union the preservation of party control has always been a more important goal than responding to the needs or wishes of the people.

## THE SHIRTLESS ONES

In Argentina only one elected government has served out its term in the past forty years. As a result, no domestic policies can be adopted with the certainty that they will be carried out. Indeed, few have ever been implemented.

When the political parties hold power, they generally announce liberal social objectives intended to help workers and the poor—those whom Perón called "the shirtless ones." Most of these objectives have never been achieved, and even minor reforms have often been undone by the Army.

Perón, of course, delivered on his promises to raise the wages and living conditions of the poor. But by printing more money to finance his programs, he not only created an unhealthy precedent for later governments, but planted the roots of Argentina's chronic inflation. So the gains the workers and the poor achieved have consistently been canceled out by their loss of purchasing power.

Argentina's weak political consensus makes it difficult for the system to define goals. Important groups do not agree on what the nation's goals should be, and are unwilling to compromise with one another. Furthermore a tradition of inefficiency and corruption in government makes it almost impossible to carry out policies intended to achieve the goals that are finally agreed upon.

## FOREIGN POLICY GOALS

In the foreign policies of democratic and authoritarian governments alike, there is a conflict between idealistic goals and realistic ones. Most nations believe they have a mission in the world. In the days of empire, the British justified colonialism as "the white man's burden"—that is, the burden of converting to Christianity and educating the less developed peoples of the world. Americans believed that they had a "manifest destiny" to dominate this continent. At the time of World War I, many Americans claimed that the mission of the United States was to "make the world safe for democracy." Argentines, too, see their country as the dominant power on their continent, and they express a kind of "manifest destiny" of their own, threatening to reclaim territories they say were taken from them by Britain, Chile, Uruguay, and Brazil. And the Russians profess the goal of world revolution. They believe they must support and encourage communist revolutions worldwide in order to overthrow the capitalists and create an international, classless society. These are all examples of idealistic goals—goals related to a nation's image of itself and to the principles for which it stands.

At the same time, all political systems must deal with certain inescapable realities—the need for security and food, for example. Such realities dictate realistic and practical goals that may very well conflict with idealistic goals.

# THE BATTLE
# FOR THE FALKLANDS

The conflict between realism and idealism was apparent in the foreign policy of each of the four nations during the battle for the Falkland Islands.

For the Argentines, realism dictated not war, but an emphasis on the problems of a near-bankrupt economy. But economic conditions had become so bad by March 1982 that there were demonstrations by workers, professionals, and the poor. Standing before the presidential palace, the mob shook their fists and called for an end to military government. The police killed two demonstrators and wounded five others. Three days later the military launched its invasion of the Falklands.

Losing its grip on the country, Argentina's junta decided on war, which it knew would unite the country behind it in a patriotic cause.

But the junta made a fatal blunder in miscalculating the position of the United States. Under Presidents Carter and Reagan, American policy toward Argentina has taken two different forms. Carter emphasized human rights in his foreign policy, saying that the United States has the duty to promote democratic ideals throughout the world. To pressure the Argentines on their human rights violations, Carter denied the junta the trade and aid it desired.

President Reagan reversed this policy, saying that the realities of American security dictate friendship and mutual-defense agreements between the United States and Argentina. The president's policy, as well as other signals from Washington, may have led the junta to believe that the U.S. would stay out of any conflict over the Falklands.

When the Argentines invaded, American decision makers were faced with a conflict between the desire to improve relations with Argentina, and a traditional friendship and alliance with Britain, with whom the United States shares a respect for democratic ideals. Although the Reagan administration first tried to act as peacemaker between the two countries, public opinion overwhelmingly supported the British cause. When negotiations broke down, the United States committed itself to supporting Britain.

## THE BRITISH AND
## RUSSIAN DILEMMAS

Britain, too, was faced with an agonizing choice. The Falklands were a residue of the empire Britain had long ago abandoned. Realistically, Britain could not afford a war over the islands. And realistically, they were of little value to Britain.

In response to the invasion, Prime Minister Thatcher sent a task force to recapture the islands. Thatcher argued that the response was justified by both idealistic and realistic considerations. A military dictatorship, she said, had deprived British subjects of their freedom. If Britain took no stand, then the cause of freedom would be weakened throughout the world. Realistically, Thatcher argued that if Britain failed to defend the Falklands, Spain might be encouraged to seize Gibraltar, which Britain considers vital to its security.

Thatcher won the solid support of British public opinion, giving her virtually a free hand in the conduct of the war. But when the British had won the Falklands, the public began to say, "If they were worth dying for, they're worth keeping." In other words, the public support that enabled Thatcher to direct an effective attack may have locked the government into the position of having to defend the islands for years. In the foreign policies of democracies, public opinion can be a source of strong, effective policy. But it can pose serious restrictions on leaders, inhibiting their flexibility.

For the Soviet Union the Falklands conflict also presented a dilemma. In need of grains to make up for its own poor harvests, the Russians had turned to Argentina. Their agreement to do business with Argentina went against everything the Soviets profess in their foreign policy. For years they had denounced the junta as fascist, just as the junta had long denounced the Russians for their communism and atheism.

But realism forced both the Russians and the Argentines to ignore their ideals. When the war broke out, the Russians faced a possible disruption of grain supplies. They warned both Britain and the United States of the dangers of intervention but remained aloof from the struggle. For their part, the British were careful not to interfere with Russian shipping, which would have given the Soviet Union reason to enter the conflict.

Some observers believe that the war may result in driving Russia and Argentina into each other's arms, as Russia seeks more grain and Argentina more currency. The developing relationship between anticommunist Argentina and antifascist Russia is a vivid reminder that nations seldom enjoy the luxury of living by their ideals.

## AN OVERVIEW

Both the British and the American systems are designed to allow voters, parties, and groups to define goals that suit the majority of the people. The process is awkward, time-consuming, and inefficient. Various groups always enjoy disproportionate power and influence. Yet over the long run, the goals and policies that win out have to have broad popular support. They must represent a consensus among many or most groups and individuals.

In both the Soviet Union and Argentina, one group defines national goals. In the Soviet Union, the Communist Party justifies its monopoly on decision making by claiming to be the only true interpreter of Marxism-Leninism, which is considered to be the only true explanation of history. Marxism-Leninism provides an unchanging blueprint for Soviet goals and policies, even though many people, including communists, believe that much of Marxism-Leninism is outdated and irrelevant. In Argentina, the armed forces define goals that are designed to further their own interests and those of two other elites—the industrialists and the landowners. In neither system do rulers believe the people are fit to define their own interests and goals.

# IV

*Conclusion*

# 12

## Democracy or Authoritarianism?

*...Government of the people,*
*by the people, for the people,*
*shall not perish from the earth.*

*Abraham Lincoln,*
*Gettysburg Address, 1863*

*We have buried the putrid corpse*
*of liberty.*

*Benito Mussolini, 1927*

**T**he American Civil War was a milestone not only in the history of the United States, but in the history of democracy. For that event revealed—for all the world to see and study—the central dilemma of democracy. Abraham Lincoln expressed that dilemma in these words:

> It has long been a grave question whether any government not too strong for the liberties of its people, can be strong enough to maintain its existence in great emergencies.

The framers of the Constitution had devised a system that would prevent the concentration and abuse of power. "In questions of power," said Jefferson, "let no more be heard of 'confidence in men.' But bind him down from mischief by the chains of the Constitution." As president of the United States during the Civil War, Lincoln found that such constitutional safeguards as the separation of powers deprived him of some of the powers he needed in order to wage the war effectively—to save the Union.

But Lincoln boldly overstepped his powers, ignoring the Senate's constitutional right to consultation, for example. Unlike President Nixon, who overstepped presidential powers during a later war, Lincoln did not assert that his actions were legal simply because he was president. Although he was convinced that he had taken the right course, he remained troubled:

> I do the very best I know how—the very best I can; and I mean to keep doing so until the end. If the end brings me out all right, what is said against me won't amount to anything. If the end brings me out wrong, ten angels swearing I was right would make no difference.

In the end, of course, Lincoln was vindicated. A government "not too strong for the liberties of its people" proved strong enough to survive. But the dilemma did not go away. In the 1930s British democracy was presented with a similar challenge.

In those years it was clear to many persons, including Conservative Party notable Winston Churchill, that Adolf Hitler was preparing Germany for war against France and Great Britain. Yet in one election after another, the British elected peace candidates who opposed rearming to meet the Nazi threat. They believed it was possible to do business with Hitler. As a result, Britain was unprepared for the war that came in 1939, and very nearly defeated during its early months.

## WHY DEMOCRACY?

Democracies are not always the most efficient or wisest form of government. In their safeguards against power, they often hamper effective leadership. In their provisions for majority rule, they sometimes prevent the adoption of the wisest course of action.

Even the ancient Greeks, who invented democracy and preferred it to oligarchy or tyranny, believed that a philosopher-king would make the best ruler. Being wise, he would not abuse his power. Being all powerful, he could rule more effectively than a group or the people.

Like the ancient Greeks, the early American democrats feared that the people might not prove wise enough to govern themselves. But the Americans preferred democracy to any other form of government because, as Jefferson put it, the people are "the most honest and safe, although not the most wise, depository of the public interests." The people, in other words, can best define their own goals.

As for the wisdom of the people, or their lack of it, the American democrats had a simple solution—education. Through public education, free speech, and freedom of the press, they believed, the people could become wise and well informed enough to govern themselves effectively. Jefferson wrote:

> Enlighten the people generally, and tyranny and oppressions of body and mind will vanish like evil spirits at the dawn of day.

The belief that democracy can work rests upon two assumptions: first, that the people can become competent and enlightened enough to govern themselves; second, that no person or group, including the majority, has a monopoly on the truth. Instead, every idea and policy must prove its value in free competition with other ideas and policies.

—*111*

Justice Oliver Wendell Holmes, Jr., expressed the reasoning behind the second premise in a decision he wrote for the Supreme Court in 1919:

> When men have realized that time has upset many fighting faiths, they may come to believe... that the best test of truth is the power of the thought to get itself accepted in the competition of the market, and that truth is the only ground upon which their wishes safely can be carried out. That at any rate is the theory of our Constitution. It is an experiment, as all life is an experiment.

If it is to work, a democratic system requires enlightened citizens who take a practical approach to politics — an approach in which ideas must compete for favor and acceptance. Government's role is to ensure the competition of ideas by upholding such rights as free speech and assembly and freedom of the press.

## AUTHORITARIAN PREMISES

Authoritarian systems rest on quite different assumptions. At the very outset, authoritarians reject the notion that the people are capable of self-government. Benito Mussolini expressed the authoritarian assumption bluntly:

> Fascism denies that the majority, by the simple fact that it is a majority, can direct human society. It denies that numbers alone can govern by means of a periodical consultation. And it affirms the unchangeable and beneficial inequality of mankind, which can never be permanently leveled....

The assumption that the people are incompetent to govern leads authoritarians to a further assumption: that is, that the government should strive not to enlighten the people, but to manipulate them into supporting the government, using any means available. Hitler perfected a technique he called "the big lie," saying, "The great masses of the people will more easily fall victim to a big lie than to a small one." Using this technique, Argentina's junta reported victories in the Falklands, even though Argentines could hear contrary reports from radio stations in nearby Uruguay.

—*112*

Authoritarians reject the premise that the best and truest polic es emerge from the conflict and competition of ideas. They believe that they alone possess the truth. Karl Marx, for example, believed that he had discovered and proved the truth of the class struggle:

> What was new on my part was to prove (1) that the existence of social classes is connected with certain historical struggles that arise out of the development of production; (2) that class struggle leads necessarily to the dictatorship of the working class; (3) that this dictatorship is only a transition to the abolition of all classes and to a classless society.

In the Soviet Union, the Communist Party enforces Marx's "truth," while suppressing all contrary theories and beliefs. The party justifies its monopoly of power by claiming to be the one true interpreter of Marx and Lenin.

The differences between democracy and authoritarianism boil down to a sharp disagreement over the intelligence of the people. Authoritarianism reflects the conviction that the people can never acquire the intellectual skills required to govern themselves. "Democracy," as journalist E. B. White put it, "is the suspicion that more than half the people are right more than half the time."

# For Further Reading

Charques, R.D. *A Short History of Russia*. New York: E.P. Dutton, 1958. (A brief and engrossing narrative that covers Russian history from the era of Kiev through the Bolshevik Revolution.)

Finer, S.E. *Comparative Government*. Baltimore: Penguin Books, 1970. (A broad introduction to comparative government that includes chapters on the Soviet Union, the United States, Britain, and the Latin American military regimes.)

Pendle, George. *A History of Latin America*. Baltimore: Penguin Books, 1963. (A readable review of Latin American history and politics, including chapters on Argentina from colonial times through Perón.)

Reeves, Richard. *An American Journey*. New York: Simon & Schuster, 1982. A journalist retraces de Tocqueville's journey of 1831–32, talking with the people and testing the validity of de Tocqueville's insights.

Rossiter, Clinton. *Six Characters in Search of a Republic*. New York: Harcourt Brace Jovanovich, 1964. (Profiles of six colonists, including Ben Franklin, emphasizing their ideas on government.)

Sampson, Anthony. *The Changing Anatomy of Britain*. New York: Random House, 1983. A fascinating journalistic account of British society and institutions, including politics and the political system.

Smith, Hedrick. *The Russians*. New York: Times Books, 1976. First-hand report on the people and the system by a former Moscow correspondent of *The New York Times*.

Woodward, E.L. *History of England*. New York: Harper & Row, 1962. (A brief, engrossing account of English history from Roman times through World War I.)

Zinn, Ricardo. *Argentina: A Nation at the Crossroads of Myth and Reality*. New York: Robert Speller & Sons, 1979. Original and profound insights on Argentine society and politics after Perón.

# Index

EATON RAPIDS
HIGH SCHOOL LIBRARY